THE MASTER LECTURE SERIES

Volume 2

Psychology and the Law

MASTER LECTURE SERIES

Psychology and the Law
Self-Study Instrument

NOW AVAILABLE

If you were unable to attend and receive credit for the 1982 Master Lecture Series on Psychology and the Law, you may obtain 10 hours of Continuing Education Credit through a self-study instrument developed to accompany this volume. For further information, please write or phone:

Psychology-Law SSI
CE Program Office
American Psychological Association
1200 Seventeenth St., N.W.
Washington, D.C. 20036
(202) 955-7719

THE MASTER LECTURE SERIES

Volume 2

Psychology and the Law

Edited by
C. James Scheirer
and
Barbara L. Hammonds

1982 MASTER LECTURERS

Donald N. Bersoff
Shari Seidman Diamond
John Monahan
David L. Rosenhan
Bruce D. Sales

AMERICAN PSYCHOLOGICAL ASSOCIATION
WASHINGTON, D.C.

Library of Congress Cataloging in Publication Data
Main entry under title:
Psychology and the law.
    (Master lecture series; v. 2)
    Bibliography
    1. Psychologists—Legal status, laws, etc.—United
States—Addresses, essays, lectures. 2. Mental health
laws—United States—Addresses, essays, lectures.
3. Psychology, Forensic—Addresses, essays, lectures.
I. Scheirer, C. James, 1941–. II. Hammonds,
Barbara L., 1943–. III. Bersoff, Donald N.
IV. Series. [DNLM: 1. Forensic psychiatry—Congresses.
2. Criminal psychology—Congresses. 3. Mental
disorders—Legislation—Congresses. 4. Psychology—
Legislation—Congresses. 5. Jurisprudence—Congresses.
W 740 P9737 1982]
KF2910.P75P74 1983   340'.11   83-11889
ISBN 0-912704-79-9

Copies may be ordered from:
Order Department
American Psychological Association
1200 Seventeenth Street, N.W.
Washington, D.C. 20036

Published by the American Psychological Association, Inc.,
1200 Seventeenth Street, N.W., Washington, D.C. 20036
Copyright 1983 by the American Psychological Association.

Printed in the United States of America.

CONTENTS

PREFACE

A t its annual convention in 1974, the American Psychological Association introduced the Master Lecture Series, a series of lectures presented by outstanding scholars and designed to provide a forum for the presentation of theory and research in selected areas of psychology. Each year five lectures focus on topics of social and ethical importance and of broad interest to the profession. At the presentation the audience is invited to participate in a discussion of these issues.

As one of the Association's most prestigious and significant activities, the series attracts large audiences at the APA Convention. It also reaches a broad audience through the distribution of tapes of the lectures and, more recently, through the production of an edited volume of Master Lecture papers. This volume, *Psychology and the Law,* is the second in the series of bound volumes derived from the Master Lecture presentations.

The Master Lecture Series was initiated and organized by the Committee on Program Innovations of the Board of Convention Affairs. This committee sponsored the series from 1974 through 1976. When the Continuing Education Committee of the Education and Training Board was established in 1976, it was given responsibility for administering the Master Lecture Series. That stewardship began with the 1977 series.

Titles for the Master Lecture Series have included the following:

Physiological Psychology (1974)
Developmental Psychology (1975)
Behavioral Control (1976)
Brain-Behavior Relationships (1977)
Psychology of Aging (1978)
Sex and Gender in Psychology (1979)
Cognitive Psychology (1980)
Psychotherapy Research and Behavior Change (1981)
Psychology and the Law (1982)

In 1983 the title for the Master Lecture Series will be *Psychology and Health,* and in 1984 it will be *Psychology and Learning.*

Psychology and the Law

Presented at the 1982 APA Convention in Washington, D.C., the papers in this volume are the work of five leading scholars in psychology and the law: Bruce Sales, Donald Bersoff, David Rosenhan, Shari Seidman Diamond, and John Monahan. These scholars probe the increasingly complex interaction of law and psychology and present two major themes: the increased regulation affecting the science and practice of psychology and the many ways in which psychology illuminates the behavioral assumptions inherent in the legal system.

In the first chapter Sales explores the impact of the legal system on the organization, allocation, and delivery of psychological services and the influence of psychological knowledge on the legal system. He discusses the validity of the behavioral assumptions underlying the present legal regulation of psychology and provides a rationale for advocacy on the part of psychologists to influence the future regulation of psychology. His paper thus provides a conceptual model from which to view the reciprocal influences of law and psychology.

Bersoff investigates the legal regulation of psychological assessment in education and employment. He discusses the regulatory effect of case and statute law on the development, validation, and use of psychological tests. He also shows that, by assuming a regulatory stance with regard to psychological testing, the legal system has forced psychologists to examine even more closely than usual questions of validity in intelligence tests, employment tests, and minimal competency examinations for graduation.

Rosenhan focuses on areas in which practitioners and research psychologists contribute to legal goals. He discusses, as examples of psychology informing the legal system, the development of definitions of psychological abnormality, the problems of psychological prediction and its implications for custody decisions, the right to refuse treatment, and the psychotherapist's obligations to clients.

Diamond discusses the inconsistency of criminal-court decisions as a framework for her exploration of the law's use of psychological knowledge. She details the role of psychology in examining the effects of jury size and composition, conformity processes, and attributional causes of behavior on jury decisions. She examines research on the extent of inconsistency in criminal justice decisions, on the sources of that inconsistency, and on efforts to reduce disparity in criminal-court decisions.

Monahan, in the final paper in the volume, examines the concept of dangerousness and its implications for the criminal justice system and for psychology. Early research on predicting violent behavior indicated that mental health professionals could predict individual behavior only poorly; a second generation of research and thought on the topic has focused on the correlates of violent behavior. According to Monahan, the 1990s are likely to see little change in the reliance of the mental health system on predictions of violence but significant change by the criminal justice system.

The thrust of these papers is that the interaction between law and psychology will increase. This interaction will be reciprocal, with the law increasingly regulating psychologists in their practice and research and with psychology offering insights into human behavior, which will be of value to the criminal- and civil-justice system.

We are indebted to the Continuing Education Committee, including Clyde Crego, Ursula Delworth, Lucia Gilbert, Kurt Salzinger, and Carl Thoresen, for the selection of timely topics and preeminent lecturers for this series. We also thank our contributors, whose cooperation in submitting excellent first drafts made our job less formidable than it might have been. Their diligence and thoughtfulness are much appreciated.

Finally, special thanks are due Anne Rogers of the Educational Affairs Office for her editorial assistance, Rosemary Beiermann of the Continuing Education Program Office for assistance in preparing materials for the Master Lecture Series and for this volume, and Brenda Bryant, APA's Manager of Special Publications, for valuable technical assistance.

C. James Scheirer
Barbara L. Hammonds

BRUCE D. SALES

THE LEGAL REGULATION OF PSYCHOLOGY: SCIENTIFIC AND PROFESSIONAL INTERACTIONS

B ruce D. Sales, a fellow of the American Psychological Association, is professor of psychology and director of the Law–Psychology Program at the University of Arizona. In 1973 while at the University of Nebraska at Lincoln, he founded the first fully integrated JD–PhD training program in law and psychology. Sales also initiated the first postdoctoral training program in this area for psychologists and lawyers. His research and writing has been supported by such agencies as the National Institute of Mental Health, the National Science Foundation, the National Institute of Justice, and the Department of Health and Human Services.

Sales has published nine books on the law-psychology interface and is working on *The Law of Psychology*, to be published by the American Psychological Association. Two of his books, *Psychology in the Legal Process* and *American Trial Judges*, have been chosen as selections by the Lawyers' Literary Club. He has written approximately 75 articles, book chapters, and monographs and has edited several special issues on law and psychology for scholarly journals.

Sales is editor of the journal *Law and Human Behavior*, editor of the book series *Perspectives in Law and Psychology*, and coeditor of the book series *Law, Society and Policy*. A past president of the American Psychology–Law Society, Sales has been an officer for several national organizations, including the American Psychological Association and the American Bar Association. He has served on task forces, boards, committees, and commissions for both organizations and is a director of APA's Division 41 (Psychology and Law).

BRUCE D. SALES

THE LEGAL REGULATION OF PSYCHOLOGY: SCIENTIFIC AND PROFESSIONAL INTERACTIONS

B ecause this edition of the Master Lecture Series considers relationships between law and psychology, I begin with a conceptual schema describing how these distinct disciplines are integrated. This model demonstrates that the legal regulation of psychology, also called the law of psychology, is a critical aspect of this interface but one relatively ignored in the explosion of research and writing. This model will also demonstrate that the study of this topic requires the involvement of both scientists and practitioners.

An Introduction to the Law–Psychology Interface

Definitions

When we speak of the integration of psychology with the law, we are most often considering psychology as a science studying the law, as a profession contributing to the legal process, or as a science and profession affected by the law. In all cases the definition of law is critical, and thus the starting point. For the purpose of this paper, *the Law* (hereinafter the Law) refers to all laws, legal systems, and legal processes.

Laws. Laws in general include all federal, state, and local laws whether derived from a constitution (constitutional law), a legislative statute (statutory law), a court decision (case law or common law), an administrative agency ruling promulgated under authority delegated by a legislature or the U.S. Congress, or a local or municipal ordinance. Although these carry different weight and effect when in conflict with one another, all are properly defined as law.

Legal systems. Legal systems are created and operated according to a law. These systems include all federal agencies such as the Department of Health and Human Services, the Department of Energy, the National Institute of Mental Health, and the National Science Foundation. This category also includes all agencies of state or local government such as the state court system and departments of mental health, education, welfare, and law enforcement.

Legal processes. Legal processes are the ways in which people are passed through or participate within legal systems according to the law. Some observers might want to eliminate this category because its scope and functions could be subsumed within the first two categories. Considering legal processes separately, however, forces us to focus on the manner in which professionals and clients are treated rather than simply on the technical letter of the law or the structure and formal operation of a system.

Behavioral Assumptions in the Law

Having defined the scope of the Law, let us turn to psychology. In Figure 1 the term *behavioral assumptions* is listed under Law. Those assumptions are the primary nexus between the two fields. Virtually all Law is based on assumptions about how people act and how these actions can be controlled. On one hand, although lawyers are equipped to draft legal language, their training is not adequate for them either to identify behavioral assumptions or to study their validity (Special Commission on the Social Sciences of the National Science Board, 1969). On the other hand, psychologists are well qualified for the task of identifying invalid assumptions and inappropriateness in the Law through the process of empirical inquiry. When behavioral assumptions are valid, psychologists can monitor and evaluate whether the Law is achieving its behavioral goals or producing unintended consequences. Finally, psychologists can provide the expertise to ensure that, wherever possible, the Law operates according to its underlying assumptions about behavior. Unquestionably psychologists could contribute meaningfully to the creation and implementation of public and legal policy.

Laws. Let us consider examples of behavioral assumptions within each of the three categories of the Law. An example of the first category, laws, is the case law that holds that juveniles arrested for a crime must

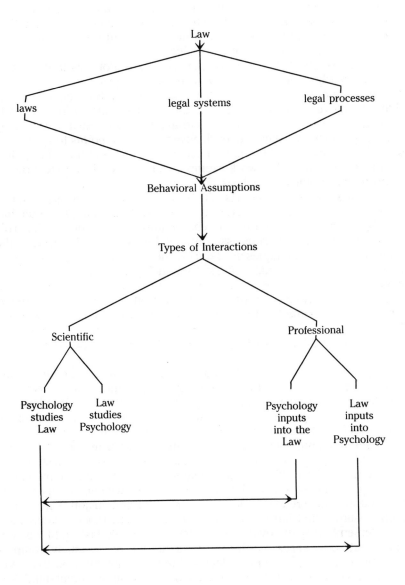

Figure 1. A model for integrating law and psychology.

be told their rights, that is, given a Miranda warning. The policy underlying this law admirably posits that juveniles, like adults, have serious interests at stake when involved in the criminal justice system and thus they should be told their rights in order to prevent their waiving them either inadvertently or out of ignorance.

As Grisso (1981) has argued, this law is based on assumptions that are not clearly articulated and whose validity needs to be assessed. These assumptions include the ideas that juveniles will understand the rights being read, remember them, and logically and rationally apply what they have heard to their situations. Grisso's research forcefully demonstrates the weakness of each assumption and points to the necessity of carefully rethinking and possibly restructuring how this policy goal is implemented. His work exemplifies the potential applications of rigorous psychological analysis and research to the law.

Legal systems. The courts illustrate how behavioral assumptions underlie the creation and operation of legal systems. A litigant often has the right to a jury trial in order to ensure fairness and impartiality. This right derives from numerous assumptions. Jury selection is based on the assumption that techniques used during the voir dire will produce a jury that is neutral at the outset of the trial. In fact many experienced trial lawyers take great pride in their ability to select juries and fill legal journals with articles based on their personal experiences (Adkins, 1968–1969; Appleman, 1968; Bodin, 1954; Darrow, 1936; Davis & Wiley, 1965; Field, 1965; Goldstein, 1938; Harrington & Dempsey, 1969; Katz, 1968–1969; Rothblatt, 1966; Shepherd, 1964–1965; Tate, Hawrish, & Clark, 1974).

Studies of attorney-conducted voir dire as a means of eliminating incompetent or biased jurors, however, suggest that this procedure is not effective (Broeder, 1965; Zeisel & Diamond, 1978). If most lawyers, and arguably judges, are unable to weed out prejudiced jurors, then the assumption that the voir dire produces a fair jury is invalid.

Even if the impaneled jury were neutral and fair-minded at the outset, validating the first assumption, other assumptions are questionable. For example, the jury's task is to listen to the evidence, remember it accurately, and reach a verdict by weighing the evidence in light of the law that the judge reads to the jury at the trial's conclusion. This assignment assumes that jurors will understand and remember the evidence.

Remembering the evidence may seem a simple task until we consider that some cases require the presentation of extremely complex information, such as economic fact and theory in an antitrust case. Will the average juror with only a high-school education understand this evidence? Some cases require 6 months or more merely to present all the evidence. Is it possible to remember every material fact presented in such a case? Common sense would argue not.

Second, it is assumed that jurors understand the law as it applies to their decision-making task. Research has shown this assumption to be incorrect. Jurors often do not understand and instead create their own rules on which to reach a verdict, rules based on their personal sense of justice or, more accurately, whim, sympathy, and prejudice (Elwork, Sales, & Alfini, 1977, 1982). Third, it is assumed that jurors reach a verdict based on the evidence presented at the trial, but numerous studies have shown that jurors use extralegal factors (see, generally, Sales, 1981). Like laws, legal systems are created and operated on the basis of suppositions about behavior, with the validity of the assumptions typically but incorrectly taken for granted.

Legal process. To illustrate how assumptions about behavior underlie legal processes, let us consider an individual who is alleged to be mentally ill and dangerous and, because of these allegations, is the subject of an involuntary civil commitment petition. The law guarantees this individual rights of due process from the time the petition is filed until the time the individual is released, assuming that he or she is committed to an institution. These rights include the right to counsel and the right to present and cross-examine witnesses.

Yet, as the previous example illustrated, the legal system does not always operate as planned. How could this affect the individual passing through the mental health system pursuant to law? One example is that of subjects of civil commitment petitions who do not always have the opportunity to exercise their rights rigorously. This situation occurs because these people often cannot fully understand their rights. And to make matters worse, if these individuals are indigent, they rarely see their attorneys for more than a few minutes before the case begins and these attorneys do not always defend their clients vigorously during trials (Poythress, Jr., 1978; Wexler, 1981).

If a person is committed, it is also assumed that he or she will receive appropriate therapy.[1] But numerous cases have demonstrated that commitment to an institution may mean custodial care without therapy (see, for example, *O'Connor v. Donaldson*, 1975). The legal process, like legal systems and laws, is based on behavioral assumptions whose validity must be empirically assessed if we are ever to improve the operation of the Law.

---

[1]Because the standard for commitment has changed during the 1970s from mental illness and the need to be hospitalized to mental illness and dangerousness, the police power of the state has been added to the parens patriae power as a justification for commitment. Under the later theory, treatment is warranted. Under the former, protection of society, and therefore custodial care, is a justifiable basis for commitment. Although the Supreme Court has not spoken on this issue, it seems reasonable that if the parens patriae power is invoked as even a partial rationale for state action, then treatment should be made available (see Wexler, 1981, for further discussion of this issue).

The Impact of Psychology on the Law

Because assumptions about behavior underlie the Law, and because the scientific study of behavior is within the domain of psychology, it follows that psychologists should be concerned with the Law. In order to mirror the structure of psychology, I suggest two categories of concern: scientific and professional.

Scientific practice. As Figure 1 notes, the scientific interaction of psychology and law has two aspects. First, psychology is a science that can be applied to the Law or, more precisely, to the study of the behavioral assumptions on which Law is based. Most, if not all, subfields of psychology will eventually contribute to this process. The recent explosion in scientific research about the Law has already covered cognitive psychology, including studies of perception (Wells, 1980), memory (Loftus, 1979), and language (Elwork et al., 1982); social psychology (Carroll & Perlman, 1978; Diamond, 1979; Greenberg & Ruback, 1982; Konĕcni & Ebbesen, 1982; Saks & Hastie, 1978; Sales, 1981), developmental psychology (Melton, Koocher, & Saks, 1983; Grisso, 1981), personality psychology (Bray & Noble, 1978), clinical psychology (Roesch & Golding, 1980; Monahan, 1981; Shah, 1981, 1978), and counseling psychology (Feldman & Wilson, 1981).

This research typically follows the model in Figure 2 or a variation of the model. The researcher identifies the legal issue that is the focus of the study, then the behavioral assumptions underlying the issue. For each assumption the researcher reviews the literature for studies that have directly tested the validity of the assumption within the legal context under question. If there are no studies or the results are inconclusive, the researcher reviews indirectly related research. Often these other studies have manipulated relevant independent or dependent variables within another contest, and thus they may provide a reasonable basis for an hypothesis about the assumption's validity.

Based on the literature review and individual goals, the researcher either plans and carries out new research, suggests a design for future research, and proceeds to the next step, or proceeds directly to the next step. This next step is to compare research findings to each identified behavioral assumption. Conclusions about the validity are made and

---

1 Examine the Law and identify the legal issue
2 Identify the behavioral assumption(s)
3 Review the existing research relevant to the validity of (2)
4 Conduct new research directly relevant to (2)
5 Assess the likelihood that each assumption (2) is valid
6 Determine the appropriateness of (1) given conclusions of (5)
7 Recommend revision of (1)

Figure 2. A model for scientific research and writing on the Law.

then weighed against the original Law and its goals. Finally, from these comparisons may come recommendations for revising the Law to conform more closely with behavioral reality. At the least, if the Law is to endure unchanged, the public should hear an honest appraisal of what it does and does not accomplish.

There are variants of this model. For some psychologists the critical issue is not the Law but a psychological theory that they wish to study. In this case the Law becomes simply another testing ground for the theory. If the research is designed to maximize external validity (Diamond, 1979), then the model in Figure 2 is still appropriate, but as an addition to the traditional psychological approaches of theory formulation, hypothesis generation, research, comparison of the results to the theory, refinement, or validation of the theory.[2] For other psychologists the goal is to study a behavioral phenomenon. Again, if the research design has high external validity, this model is adaptable with only minor adjustments.

Another type of scientific interaction applies the Law, in particular legal theory and procedure, to the study of psychology. Of all the interconnections between Law and psychology, this is the least well developed. Examples include researchers using legal theory to generate hypotheses about group behavior and comparing the Law's adversarial model of truth seeking to psychology's scientific model for discovery (Levine, 1974).[3]

Professional service delivery. Let us consider the professional interconnections between psychology and the Law. As professionals, psychologists regularly contribute to the Law. The most common instance is the psychologist's being asked to testify in court. For example, clinical and counseling psychologists are employed by courts or parties to evaluate and testify about defendants who allege insanity when a crime was committed. Professional psychologists have testified in many other proceedings, both criminal (e.g., sexual sociopathy, incompetency to stand trial, sentencing) and civil (e.g., child custody, workers' compensation, vocational disability, involuntary civil commitment). Most often these

---

[2]This approach is not meant to imply that research using the model in Figure 2 is not theoretical. Although the Law is the first step, and its study the goal, theory is part of step 4—generating researchable hypotheses—and the findings are a test of the theory. Furthermore, findings as to how the Law operates may be used to construct a theory of behavior in legal contexts (e.g., Konečni & Ebbesen, 1981); this would occur during a new step (8) in the model.

[3]Some of Wexler's writings (Wexler, 1980; 1981, chapter 7) also appear to fit this category. Wexler argued that the law requiring therapists to protect the potential victim from a client's potentially dangerous behavior may actually make successful therapeutic outcomes more likely by increasing the use of family or joint therapy between the client and the potential victim. The impact of legal intervention on the process and outcome of therapy is a rich avenue for psychological research and has led David S. Hargrove and me to speculate that the phrase *psycholegal therapeutic intervention* may become a recognized construct in clinical psychology.

situations involve a psychologist whose primary identification is as a professional rather than as a scientist, but psychologists who are primarily scientists also act as experts in court cases.

The relationship between psychologists acting in this professional capacity and the science of psychology does not end with scientific testimony in court. The *Ethical Principles of Psychologists* (APA, 1981), the *Standards for Providers of Psychological Services (APA, 1977)*, and the *Specialty Guidelines for the Delivery of Services* (APA Committee on Professional Standards, 1981) require psychologists to be familiar with the scientific research relevant to the issues about which they testify. The professional role of psychologists with regard to the law thus depends on their remaining current as scientists.

As professionals, psychologists are involved with the Law in other ways, such as evaluators, consultants, or therapists employed by a legal agency. The limitations of this volume preclude discussion of these roles in more depth.[4]

The Impact of the Law on Psychology

The other side of the professional interaction is the impact of Law on psychology, that is, the legal regulation or the Law of psychology. This area has received little attention in either the legal or psychological literature, especially compared to the volume dedicated to psychology as a science that studies the Law or as a profession that provides expert services to the Law.[5]

An obvious reason for the dearth of scholarship is that psychologists are rarely equipped to find and analyze the law. As with the acquisition of any skill, this deficiency can be overcome. But another reason may be that the law is not important to most psychologists. Forman and Shackar (1981) present this argument. They disagree with psychologists who have recently argued for legislative lobbying to achieve laws favorable to psychologists and psychology, suggesting that the psychology profession undertakes such efforts because it is jealous of the medical community, and that if one wished to train "real doctors," the simple and obvious solution would be to issue cadavers to all doctoral students in professional psychology.

Although offered in jest, their proposal actually works against their point, illustrating how important it is to understand the law of psychol-

[4]The information and expertise that psychology provides the Law can also be organized by legal categories such as criminal law, commercial law, and environmental law. Within each category would be organized all the related scientific information that psychologists can provide, as well as the roles that psychologists could play to aid in the administration of the law under that category.
[5]For examples of excursions into this area see Hogan (1979), Knapp and Vandecreek (1982, 1981), and Schwitzgebel and Schwitzgebel (1980).

ogy. A colleague and I (Overcast & Sales, 1982) checked into the matter and found many state laws that regulate the donation and sale of cadavers and body parts, some so restrictively that Forman and Shackar's solution would require major legislative action. Only nine states make no attempt to specify who may legally accept donations of cadavers. Forman and Shackar also fail to understand that state laws define the rights and duties of recipients legally in possession of a cadaver. And many states specifically define the procedures that can be performed on a cadaver—none permits their use in assertiveness training or flat affect studies. Even with a silly proposal, it is almost impossible to avoid considering the law's impact on psychological practice.

The remainder of this paper focuses on the law. Since this law often involves the creation and operation of legal systems and legal processes, however, all parts of the Law are at least implicitly, and often explicitly, relevant.

Understanding the Law's Mandates

To assert the importance of devoting substantial attention to the law of psychology, it is important to understand the four purposes of such study.

Upholding Standards of Ethics and Practice

First, the formal standards guiding the behavior of psychologists dictate that all scientists and professionals stay current about not only organizational standards but also legal developments that affect their work (see Principle 3 of the *Ethical Principles of Psychologists*, APA, 1981; Standard 2.2.2 and 2.2.4 of the *Standards for Providers of Psychological Services*, APA, 1977; and Guideline 2 of the *Specialty Guidelines for the Delivery of Services*, APA Committee on Professional Standards, 1981). In addition, the laws that regulate psychology cannot be ignored, for they are sanctioned by government and are the basis for private lawsuits. Finally, laws may also confer important benefits, but only if known and properly invoked.

Assessing the Impact of the Law

Second, it is necessary to examine laws to determine their impact on the conduct of science and the delivery of professional services. In studying these laws, I have distinguished four broad categories.

Scientific practice. The laws that regulate scientific practice constitute the first category. For years social science researchers have promised subjects that their responses would be held in strictest confidence. These assurances were based on both professional standards and beliefs about the law's mandates. But these promises of confidentiality are not always possible to keep, because under some conditions a researcher may be compelled by law to disclose this information to another party. Some of these conditions are implicit in the courts' subpoena power (Comment, 1977; Knerr & Carroll, 1978); researchers can be subpoenaed to present data—even when collected under assurance of confidentiality—as evidence in a legal action. Another threat to confidentiality may be the federal Freedom of Information Act (Morris, Sales, & Berman, 1981) and similar state laws, which jeopardize not only the confidential relationship with subjects but the researcher's property interests in the data as well.[6] Other examples in this category are laws regulating animal experimentation (Sales & Overcast, Note 1) and the development and use of psychological tests (Bersoff, 1981; Lerner, 1981 Overcast & Sales, Note 2).

Professional service delivery. Laws in the second category regulate the delivery of professional services. These include the licensure and certification laws that regulate the title and practice of psychology (Stigall, 1983) and the other laws that affect the professional's role in providing services (e.g., Morse, 1983; Sales, Powell, Van Duizend, & Associates, 1982). These latter laws govern, for example, the criteria for involuntary civil commitment, guardianship and conservatorship, competency to stand trial, and responsibility for the commission of a criminal act. In order for psychologists to provide services well, they must understand the legal context. For example, a psychologist asked to evaluate an individual in order to determine competency to stand trial is not being asked to determine whether that individual is mentally ill. The law has established its own definition of competency; the professional is required to direct the evaluation against the law's criteria. To apply any other standard for assessment could lead the judge to disregard the psychologist's testimony and could create serious consequences for the client.

Organization and administration of a professional business enterprise. Laws in the third category regulate the organization and administration of the profession as a business enterprise. A prime example is the group of laws that affect reimbursement for services independently provided by psychologists. Prior to state freedom-of-choice laws, which mandate that health insurance companies reimburse psychologists directly, many insurers restricted their coverage to psychiatrists or to psychologists supervised by psychiatrists. A thorough knowledge of this law, its requirements, and its structure is essential to any psychologist providing health services (Dorken, 1983).

[6]A property interest, according to *Black's Law Dictionary* (4th ed.), "means a right to have the advantage of accruing from anything . . . the exclusive right of possessing, enjoying, and disposing of a thing" (p. 1382).

Legal controls on clients. The final category includes laws that regulate the entry of clients into the service system, the processing of clients through that system, and the rights of clients during this process. In some cases these laws are part of the same statutes that regulate the professional's services. Regardless of the source of the law, the professional must understand how the law controls those aspects of the client's behavior related to the professional's services (Wexler, 1981). For example, civil commitment statutes specify the behaviors that must be present before an individual is subject to commitment, the procedures to follow to secure commitment, the place to which the person will go once committed, and the individual's rights during each stage of the process. The provider of psychological services must have this knowledge in order to initiate proceedings on behalf of a client or to respond appropriately if asked to assess or treat an individual facing commitment or to testify for or against such commitment.

As our understanding of the law of psychology becomes more sophisticated, these four categories will doubtlessly change. For now, they are a good way to organize our thinking about the law in order to determine its impact on psychology and psychologists.

Assessing the Validity of Behavioral Assumptions

Knowledge gained from accomplishing the first two purposes leads naturally to the third purpose for studying the law, that is, to identify and assess the validity of the behavioral assumptions underlying it. To illustrate, consider confidentiality and privileged communications laws (DeKraai & Sales, 1982; Note 3). Confidentiality is a broad concept that originated in professional ethics codes but today is covered by many types of statutes and by case law. A confidential communication is generally understood to mean any information known by or communicated between two or more persons, the knowledge of which is limited by law or ethics to those persons or designated individuals. Privileged communications law, a subarea of confidentiality law, came about because confidentiality law did not apply in the courts and could not protect or prevent psychologists from revealing a confidential communication when called as a witness in a legal proceeding. Most state legislatures have attempted to remedy this situation by enacting privileged communication statutes, which protect the client's confidential communications when the psychologist is called to the witness stand.[7]

[7]Privileged communications statutes may also be interpreted to impose a confidentiality requirement on communications between the psychologist and the client. Although these statutes typically contain language that refers to judicial and quasijudicial proceedings, courts have interpreted a physician privilege statute to impose a duty to keep information confidential that was gained in the course of treating a patient (e.g., *Schaffer v. Spicer,* 1974).

This law is based on a series of behavioral assumptions (Shuman & Weiner, 1982) that must be identified and tested for us to know whether the law is even necessary and, if so, to assess whether its structure is appropriate. These behavioral assumptions can be summarized as follows: Without assurance of confidentiality, many individuals will not seek psychotherapy, will delay their entry into therapy for the same reason, will be reluctant to divulge essential information during therapy, and will terminate therapy prematurely. Unfortunately the research on the validity of these assumptions is contradictory (e.g., Shuman & Weiner, 1982; Meyer & Smith, 1977; Meyer & Willage, 1980; Woods & McNamara, 1980). In addition, because these studies have methodological limitations, their findings either are of questionable accuracy or are difficult to generalize (Dekraai & Sales, 1980; Note 3). Clearly the study of the law and psychology of confidential communication, and their integration, is important from both a scientific and professional standpoint.

Informing Policy Recommendations

This leads to the fourth purpose for our attention to the law: The ability to make informed recommendations for policy changes. Having identified which laws affect psychology and having studied the behavioral assumptions underlying these laws, we are in an excellent position to recommend ways to restructure the law to make it more appropriate for psychologists and their clients.

The Law of Psychology: Major Implications

A project begun several years ago on behalf of the American Psychological Association is strengthening our knowledge of the legal regulation of psychology. Under the sponsorship of APA's Board of Professional Affairs and with the aid of colleagues and students, I undertook to review and analyze those laws that affect the professional psychologist. The process was to identify an area of law (such as professional incorporation), analyze its components, and review this law to determine how it works in each state and federal jurisdiction. The project was expanded to consider all areas of law that affect the science and profession of psychology. With this expanded focus, sponsorship of this project has moved to the APA ad hoc Committee on Legal Issues. And the first of what may be several volumes on the results will be published by APA.

Because it is not possible in this context to consider all the areas of law that affect psychology, and because most of our findings about specific laws have appeared or will appear elsewhere, the discussion here focuses on a few major analyses with broad application across several areas of law, with our review of particular laws illustrating these analyses. This conceptual schema for understanding critical issues in the law of psychology may ultimately prove more important to this area than the analysis of any particular law.

Structural Differences Within the Law

One of the first things learned during the project was that laws affecting psychology vary significantly in structure among jurisdictions. Let us consider the law of professional incorporation. Depending on an individual practitioner's circumstances, forming a corporation often offers many tax and financial liability benefits.[8] My initial assumption was that the states would treat requests from psychologists to incorporate with some uniformity, recognizing psychologists, like physicians and lawyers, as legitimate professionals entitled to benefit from this law. Examining the law, we found this assumption partially accurate. Only eight jurisdictions prohibit psychologists from incorporating while allowing other medical and mental-health–related professionals to do so. Nevertheless, why a substantial number of states do deny psychologists this benefit is an important issue to which I will return later.

It also seemed reasonable to assume that the states would have drafted similar statutes. This second assumption, however, was not supported by the analysis. Professional incorporation statutes take one of three different approaches to identify the groups eligible for incorporation (Overcast & Sales, 1981). The least restrictive provides that *any* profession that can be practiced only according to a state license may be the basis of a professional corporation. Some states in this category have established a general professional corporation statute as well as separate statutes for specific professions.

The second type of statute allows any licensed professional to incorporate but mentions certain occupations. Of the professional groups mentioned,[9] physicians, dentists, and osteopaths are most frequently cited (in 15, 15, and 13 states, respectively). Chiropractors, chiropodists, optometrists, and podiatrists are cited in at least 9 states, while psychologists, in common with naturopaths, appear only once.

Of greatest concern are the 19 states that limit professional incorporation to professions specified in the statutes. Of these states 11 refer

---

[8]A bill introduced in Congress, The Pension Equity Act (H.R. 6410), by Congressman Charles Rangel of New York in 1982 would decrease the benefits of professional incorporation. It would not, however, affect the conceptual points made in this section, for which other legal evidence is available.

[9]Chiropractors, chiropodists, dentists, physicians, optometrists, osteopaths, podiatrists, naturopaths, dispensing opticians, pharmacists, and psychologists.

to psychologists. Eight states do not and thus presumably exclude the profession from the benefits of incorporation. As might be expected, physicians, chiropractors, dentists, and optometrists are most frequently named.[10]

Since psychologists are eligible to incorporate in most jurisdictions, why should the enabling legal structure be of concern? The answer is that all statutes are open to judicial interpretation. Where the language of the statute is ambiguous, the courts may be called on to determine whether the legislature intended to include psychologists as professionals eligible to incorporate. The inability to predict how the courts will decide in any given case is all too familiar. Furthermore, the fact that a statute mentions several groups but omits psychologists may be interpreted as a negative pregnant, that is, the omission is considered pregnant with negative meaning. Finally, as sunset laws become more common, what would happen to psychologists if the state licensing law were abolished and the state professional incorporation law defined eligibility for incorporation on the basis of state licensing? Psychologists could no longer incorporate and, if already incorporated, might be forced to dissolve the corporation.

The lesson from this is that in law the means—the language and structure of a statute—are as important as the end. Attention to this lesson may save psychologists hours of work and financial expense in trying to correct a situation that a fraction of the effort would have avoided in the first place.

Complex Structuring

Let us consider another area of law, that of workers' compensation, which illustrates how complex the issue of structure can become. Psychologists are concerned with this area of law for they may need to claim a benefit because of a personal work-related injury such as an assault by a patient and because they treat clients whose injuries, whether psychological or psychologically induced, are work related.

Workers' compensation laws were designed to compensate an employee who sustains a work-related injury without considering whose fault the injury was. The legal test or formula used to determine whether

---

[10]The number in parentheses following the group name represents the number of states that specified the profession: physicians (19), chiropractors (18), dentists (17), optometrists (17), podiatrists (13), osteopaths (12), psychologists (11), nurses (9), pharmacists (8), physical therapists (7), chiropodists (6), and naturopaths (2). The following professions were mentioned only by a single state: audiologists, certified social workers, dental hygienists, electrologists, masseurs/masseuses, occupational therapists, ophthalmic dispensers, and speech pathologists.

a worker may receive compensation is that the injury must "arise out of and in the course of employment." All jurisdictions have adopted this or similar language (Merrikin, Overcast, & Sales, 1982; Sales, Overcast, & Merrikin, in press).

But what kind of injury and causation must be shown? In many early decisions under these statutes, courts adhered to the common law principle that conditions the right to compensation on a physical impact on the injured worker's body, whether or not the contact was directly related to the injury received. For example, if two workers were deafened by a boiler explosion but only one were slightly wounded by a piece of flying metal, the traditional interpretation of the law would have held that only the worker touched by the metal could receive compensation for deafness. Later decisions have recognized the inequities arising from strict adherence to the physical contact rule; courts usually condition compensation on convincing evidence of a causal relationship between the injury and the workplace.

The recognition of psychological causation and injuries has led to more complex law, best understood by the following characterization: *physical-physical injury* (a physical cause resulting in a physical injury), *physical-mental injury* (a physical cause resulting in a mental injury), *mental-physical injury* (a mental cause resulting in a physical injury), and *mental-mental injury* (a mental cause resulting in a mental injury).[11]

As my colleagues and I discovered when looking closely into this law, the complexity does not stop here. Although injuries under the first two categories are compensable in all jurisdictions so long as other requirements of the statutes are met, the remaining categories are not dealt with uniformly. For example, cases of mental-physical injuries, although compensable in almost every jurisdiction, are further subdivided on the basis of the nature of the mental stimulus. These distinguish mental stimuli of intense (stressful) but brief duration, intense and prolonged duration, and less intense but prolonged duration.

As if this were not complicated enough, by far the greatest confusion surrounds cases in which a mental stimulus has produced a mental injury, particularly if no specific blameworthy incident can be pinpointed as the cause of the mental injury. Twenty-one jurisdictions have no case law on compensation for mental-mental injuries. The states with such case law differ according to whether they deny compensation for all mental-mental claims, compensate for only sudden onset claims, or compensate for gradual onset claims as well.

Of the jurisdictions with such case law, only six specifically rule out compensation for both gradual and sudden onset mental injuries. The courts in these cases generally argue that the statutory definition of *accident* or *injury* does not encompass injuries without a physical com-

---

[11]The reader is cautioned that these categories are purely legal distinctions; they do not represent classifications recognized outside the law.

ponent. However, some courts in other states with similar statutory language have awarded compensation for mental-mental claims based on the reasoning that the mind is a part of the "human physical structure."[12]

Twenty-five jurisdictions allow compensation for mental-mental injuries of sudden onset. Courts that recognize a right to compensation when an employee suffers a mental injury as a result of a sudden, work-related stimulus reason generally that this right arises from the disabling effect on the worker, not from the nature of the injury or its cause. In these jurisdictions courts will award compensation in sudden onset mental injury cases when they find that the disabling injury was caused by the employment.

The 15 states that award compensation for gradual onset mental injuries are a subset of those recognizing sudden onset claims. While 6 of these do not distinguish between gradual and sudden onset mental injuries in defining requirements for proof of injury, the others have placed additional conditions on recovery in cases of gradual onset.

These conditions fall into three groups. First, some jurisdictions require that the harm to the claimant be objectively measurable or observable, a higher level of proof than required for sudden onset. Second, some courts condition compensation on the claimant's exposure to unusual stress or strain. Compensation is not granted for disorders brought on by ordinary day-to-day stress, even if the claimant establishes the second leg of the test, the work connection. Third, some courts will entertain claims based on ordinary stress but require the claimant to establish a casual link between the injury and the workplace based on objective evidence. Several jurisdictions combine some or all of these limitations. Despite the variations in language, all these statutes place a greater burden on the claimant seeking compensation for an injury allegedly brought on through exposure to daily work-related stress than for unusual stress.

This area of law vividly shows how substantially jurisdictions can vary in the structural complexity of their statutory approach to issues of concern to psychology and how the structure can seriously affect psychologists and their clients. This example also raises questions of why some legal structures are so complex and how we can make the law become more rational in its approach.

In the case of professional incorporation law, a lobbying effort to correct a situation probably caused by legislative oversight or sloppy legal drafting would solve many of the problems. The complex structure of workers' compensation law, however, is more likely caused by the dearth of psychological research to justify a simple approach. For instance, both courts and legislatures are well aware that mental injury claims demand the establishment of what appears to the layperson to be

[12]*Todd v. Goosetree* (1973).

an intangible injury. When faced with a compensatory scheme pregnant with possibilities for malingering, courts and legislatures have hesitated to deem the entire class of mental injuries compensable. The structure of workers' compensation will remain awkwardly complex until psychological research develops accurate techniques for identifying malingering and delineates the relationship between job pressures and mental injuries and until the legal community modifies the worker's compensation system to consider adequately the multiple causes of mental disabilities. Psychological research also is needed to address structural complexity in many other areas of law.

Impact of the Law on the Organization of Psychological Services

Law also affects the organizational structure through which a psychologist can deliver services. On one level this finding is not startling. Laws affect the business organization practices of other professionals; why should they not affect psychologists? But when a revision in the law alters an organizational structure that affects service delivery, the change may have important, unforeseen consequences.

Services in the private sphere. Let us return to professional incorporation law for an illustration. As noted, this law can confer benefits on professionals and, as examined to this point, affects business organization. But its effect was shown only in the legal sense.

An element of this law, however, can also influence the delivery of psychological services. If a psychologist chose to organize a group practice with professionals from other disciplines, such as a physician, a neurologist, a psychiatrist, and a social worker, and to incorporate this group, one might assume that the professionals felt this organization to be in their clients' interest and that the law should not stand in their way. In fact, 12 states prohibit psychologists from cross-disciplinary incorporation while granting this right to other professional groups (Overcast & Sales, 1981).

Arguably this prohibition does not restrict multidisciplinary practice because these laws permit psychologists to practice with other groups so long as they do not incorporate. But the law makes it financially disadvantageous to do so. Why should a psychologist eligible for incorporation be required to give up this status in order to work with professionals in other disciplines? Thus, because of this law at least some psychologists, and perhaps a substantial number, would be much less likely to engage in a multidisciplinary approach to service delivery. A careful examination of this law is needed to determine whether the policy implicit in its structure is appropriate for mental health professionals and conducive to the best service delivery (Kiesler, 1980).

Services in the public sphere. Laws also affect the organization of services in the public sphere, for example, those creating special mechanisms for processing sex offenders (Brunette & Sales, 1980).[13] When we reviewed the law in 1978, 24 states had sexual sociopath statutes that required evaluations and their results to be communicated to the court, which would consider this information in determining the disposition of the sex offender.[14] This disposition might include mental health treatment as well as incarceration. Periodic evaluations after incarceration were also required in some states to help the court decide whether to continue confinement or treatment. Three other states did not have statutes involving mental health professionals in disposition rulings but did involve them in the evaluation of sex offenders before parole or probation.

These laws organize the system and the process so specifically that they spell out distinctions between the responsibilities granted different classes of mental health professionals. Statutes dictate the psychologist's and psychiatrist's responsibility for conducting evaluations and providing treatment to the sex offender, the authority of these professionals to make recommendations regarding disposition of the sex offender, the authority of different professionals to administer the state institution for sex offenders, and the expendability of a profession in the process, that is, whether the participation of a psychologist or psychiatrist is required.

A review of the 27 jurisdictions revealed that responsibility and authority were statutorily vested with the psychiatric profession almost exclusively and that psychiatrists were virtually inexpendable. Psychologists, however, were thoroughly expendable. Twenty-four statutes required at least one of the evaluators to be a psychiatrist or physician, whereas none required one to be a psychologist. In 19 statutes only psychiatrists or physicians could be involved in the process. No state limited participation to psychologists.

Because these laws dictate the organization and the delivery of mental health services to individuals, we must question the underlying behavioral assumptions in order to promote the appropriate delivery of mental health care and the appropriate legal regulation of professional psychology. In this area of law there are several basic questions to address. Why did approximately half the states not consider this a mental health problem but limited treatment to the regular services provided

[13]Because my review of this law was completed in 1978, before several states reconsidered their philosophy and approach and made statutory changes, this material is presented in the past rather than the present tense. The legal changes that have occurred, however, do not affect the import, relevance, or validity of the main thesis of this section.

[14]The phrase *sexual sociopath* is used generically, since some states refer to these persons as criminal sexual psychopathic persons, mentally disordered sex offenders, sexual psychopaths, sexually dangerous persons, criminal sexual psychopathics, dangerous sexual offenders, and habitual sex offenders.

incarcerated felons? Would the therapeutic literature support this approach? Why did the majority of jurisdictions that considered sexual sociopathy a mental health problem warranting a special treatment system nevertheless find the problem exclusively medical? Why did a few states legislate equal responsibility, authority, and expendability to both psychologists and psychiatrists? Were their recommended approaches correct?

We must turn to the existing literature to determine what is known about appropriate professional roles for psychologists and psychiatrists in the evaluation and treatment of sex offenders and in the organization and administration of treatment facilities. If no literature addresses these issues, it must be generated according to the model in Figure 2. Only through scientific research can psychologists ascertain the rationality and desirability of laws affecting the organization of psychological and other professional services.[15]

Impact of the Law on the Delivery of Psychological Services

As I have noted, a law that affects the organization of professional services also can affect decisions about the allocation of roles to different types of professionals. Some laws, however, affect these decisions without speaking to organizational issues. For example, the law can create new jobs or roles for psychologists by determining that psychologists are qualified to perform a specific service within the legal system. This happened years ago when mental health professionals were first asked to testify about the competence of criminal defendants to stand trial. Since the measure of incompetence is not mental illness or any classic psychological construct, the law actually created a new role for psychologists and other mental health professionals.

In established service areas the law also allocates the defines roles. For example, psychologists have traditionally provided evaluation and therapy on a private basis to persons with sexual problems. However, when the public system was created to handle those with sexual problems who also violate criminal laws, psychologists in some states were prohibited from performing these tasks.

Discriminatory allocation of roles. By establishing roles, whether creating new roles or regulating traditional ones, the law may be dis-

---

[15]One might argue, however, that such scholarship is not needed to sway the fundamentally political decisions of a legislature. If one musters constituent support—votes and financial contributions for the legislator at election time—the legislator will follow one's wishes. This is true to some extent but not in all cases. If constituencies split on an issue, how does the legislature break the stalemate? Data may help. Perhaps most important is American psychology's scientific, data-oriented basis. Not to sustain this tradition when seeking legal change could severely undercut the profession's credibility in the long run. While others present opinions, we should present facts.

criminatory. For example, sexual sociopathy law assigns roles to psychiatrists and other physicians that are prohibited to psychologists. If this assignment were based on differences in the ability of professions to provide services, then the classification would be rational. If the law simply reflected more effective lobbying by physicians and stereotypical opinions held by some legislators as to the relative skill of physicians and psychologists, then the classification would be discriminatory.

It would be interesting to determine from historical records why legislatures and courts have created these roles and what influence psychologists and other professional groups have had in the process.[16] Scholarship could reveal whether a statute is appropriate, shed light on the science and politics of creating good law, and suggest ways that psychologists could influence the legislative process. These investigations could become the basis for new research into the acquisition and application of psychological expertise by policy makers and legal systems (see, e.g., Massad, Sales, & Acosta, 1983).

Silence on role allocation. Although there are numerous examples of legal intervention in the allocation of psychological services, the law is strangely silent on these issues in some contexts. For example, the federal Education for All Handicapped Children Act (1975) was enacted to ensure for all handicapped children a free, appropriate public education that emphasizes special education and related services designed to meet their unique educational needs. To qualify for federal assistance under the act, each state is required to demonstrate that it has developed both policies and programs to ensure that all handicapped children receive these services. The states responded by enacting statutes mandating these services, but the statutes differ considerably in their degree of specificity (Overcast & Sales, 1980). These laws reveal several several stages of the procedures in which the psychologist might play an important role in indentifying, placing, and working with children in special education programs.

Few statutes, however, recognize the psychologist's skills. Unlike other areas of law, such as the processing of sex offenders, the statutes do not discriminate against psychologists in favor of other professionals. Rather, most statutes do not mention any professions, delegating to state administrative agencies the promulgation of rules and regulations governing special education.

Although a law that is silent may be preferable to one that is discriminatory, the silence cannot be ignored. Psychologists are specifically trained to provide the kinds of insight and services called for by special education legislation. To omit any reference to this expertise in

---

[16]The same point applies to federal and state administrative agencies that commonly have the authority delegated by the legislature to write binding rules. The discussion of special education law later in this paper demonstrates that these agencies often have substantial authority to allocate roles.

the statutes only increases the likelihood that needed expertise will not be tapped.

The profession of psychology should therefore contribute more actively to the legislative process (DeLeon, 1983; DeLeon, O'Keefe, VandenBos, & Kraut, 1982; Dorken, 1981, 1983). We should educate state legislators about the skills of psychologists so as to encourage the revision of existing law to use the available psychological resources. Other approaches should be pursued, such as lobbying the administrative bodies responsible for choosing which professional groups should provide services when the relevant statute is silent or permissive on this issue. This lobbying is particularly important because statutory language commonly fails to mention psychologists specifically but is sufficiently general to permit their inclusion.

Allocation between professions. Silence on the part of the law raises another issue. Which type of professional should statutes recognize and by what criteria should this decision be made? For example, when state special education statutes mention psychologists, they do so often in the generic sense. Neither the type of psychologist nor the level of education, training, or experience that should be brought to the task is specified, nor is reference made to the licensure or certification status of the psychologist. This situation suggests yet another reason for psychology to be involved actively in the legislative process, because it is in the best position to respond to these concerns. Organized psychology, for example, should consider whether a law should specify school psychologists alone. If not, what other types of psychologists have the skills to provide the necessary services? Should recognition be reserved to psychologists licensed and certified by the state board of psychology examiners or by the state department of education, or should it be extended to some combination of these persons or others?

Nor is this issue the exclusive concern of doctoral-level psychologists. Holders of the master's degree, nonpsychologist counselors, and others are affected. Competition among providers is keen and will increase. Both guild interests and the public interest demand research that will document the psychologist's skills and compare these to other providers. The results can serve as the basis for advocating legal arrangements that appropriately utilize each type of professional's skills (Dix & Poythress, Jr., 1981).

Legislators should see psychologists as professionals who seek data to justify their positions and who present this information in an unbiased manner. Such attributions should make legislators more willing to seek out psychologists as sources of information.[17] The goal should be to increase the appropriate use of psychological resources, not to decrease the activities of allied professionals. Psychology has

---

[17]This assertion is simply that; it begs for research on the factors that affect legislators' use of behavioral and other social science information (Massad, Sales, & Acosta, 1983).

little to fear from these other professionals; the scientific base on which our professional expertise is built guarantees that our services will continue to be competitive in the marketplace.[18]

Allocation of responsibilities. We have focused on the law's involvement in the allocation of roles. But the sexual sociopath laws, for example, prescribed not c:ily roles but also responsibilities. It is helpful to distinguish these functions within the conceptual schema for the law of psychology, because statutes may focus on responsibilities without considering roles. The law of confidentiality is a good example because it defines psychologists' responsibilities concerning information gained from professional interactions with clients but not whether or how their services could be performed.

This conceptual category, like those discussed, requires scientific scrutiny to determine if the law is needed and, if so, if it is rationally structured. For example, laws relating to access to treatment records vary among states in their restrictiveness from complete access for all clients over 12 years of age to complete psychotherapist discretion. This divergence in approach is equally represented in the professional literature (e.g., Epstein et al, 1981; Schuckman, 1980; Smith, 1981). Research is needed to assess the effect of client access to records on subsequent client behavior so that a policy recommendation can be based on objective information about the impact of different legal arrangements.

Along these lines, let us consider the part of this law that states that where the therapist determines or reasonably should have determined that a client poses a serious threat to others, a duty arises to exercise reasonable care to protect the foreseeable victim (e.g., Tarasoff v. Board of Regents, 1974). One commentator has argued that

[18]As Shah (Note 5) correctly observes, whenever we are interested in a law that affects our clients, our research subjects, or ourselves, we run the risk of letting guild interests cloud our judgment, both in identifying behavioral assumptions and in interpreting the data that result from empirical assessments of these assumptions. For example, in assessing the roles of psychologists and psychiatrists in administration of the insanity defense, we found that the law still favors psychiatric involvement (Morris & Sales, in press) despite sufficient literature to conclude that there is no validity to the assumption that psychiatrists are more skilled than psychologists in this area. But does that mean that we should lobby for parity and be allowed to testify in all jurisdictions as to whether a defendant were insane at the time of the offense?

If the law chooses to request such testimony from psychiatrists, then it should recognize psychologists as well. But the public interest demands that we consider a more basic question, namely, whether any mental health professional is able to make a reasonable determination of legal insanity. Perhaps psychiatrists and psychologists should testify only on their prediction of the person's mental state at the time of the crime or other judgments directly within their expertise. The determination as to whether the person was legally insane and not responsible for her or his acts would then be left to the jury or the judge (Morse, 1983). We must be sensitive to the value judgments implicit in our involvement as scientists in studying the law of psychology and as professionals arguing for a change in that law (Simon, 1983).

The following implications for the practice of psychotherapy are immediately apparent: 1) greater numbers of patients will incriminate themselves and be subject to legal action; 2) psychotherapists may well have to defend themselves in courts of law for making allegations about patients, 3) a basically antagonistic relationship may develop between the patient and the psychotherapist, 4) therapists acting in accordance with the principle of full and informed consent may well deter patients from seeking their help, and 5) ultimately fewer and fewer people will avail themselves of psychotherapeutic services because of the fear that they may talk about the "wrong" things or express unacceptable feeling or desires. (Noll, 1976, p. 1453)

Each of these assertions, unless backed by data, becomes an hypothesis that requires empirical scrutiny. The results of such studies would allow sensible recommendations as to the appropriate structuring of the law regulating our responsibilities.

Conclusion

The above findings illustrate what can be learned from studying the Law of psychology. This information helps make apparent that this topic is an integral and significant aspect of the relationship between law and psychology. This area demands new directions for research and new initiatives for professional involvement in the legal and political arenas. I hope that these new involvements will generate more rational policies for the regulation of professional and scientific behavior and the behavior of our clients and research subjects. The benefits of studying the Law of psychology are not limited to the creation of a more appropriate legal structure. Knowledge of the Law will lead to empirical assessments of the validity of the assumptions about human behavior underlying the Law, assessments that will often entail answers to new questions and the generation of new psychological knowledge.[19]

[19]For examples of this process, refer to the research suggested regarding the laws reviewed in this paper. Studies of this law can also lead to revised organizational standards. For example, part of the impetus for revising Principle 9 relating to research with human participants of the *Ethical Principles of Psychologists* was to have it conform with the federal guidelines (Koocher, 1983). Such sensitivity and responsiveness are entirely appropriate and mandated in Principle 3 of the *Ethical Principles of Psychologists* (APA, 1981). It states:

b. As employees or employers, psychologists do not engage in or condone practices that result in illegal . . . actions. . . .

c. In their professional roles, psychologists avoid any action that will violate or diminish the legal and civil rights of clients or of others who may be affected by their actions.

This is not to argue that our professional standards must reflect legal tenets verbatim. This is impossible because laws on the same topic often vary among jurisdictions. Changing

Reference Notes

1. Sales, B. D., & Overcast, T. D. *The legal regulation of animal experimentation.* In preparation.
2. Overcast, T. D., & Sales, B. D. *State regulation of psychological tests.* In preparation.
3. Dekraai, M. B., & Sales, B. D. *Confidential communications of psychotherapists.* Submitted for publication.
4. Falk, P., & Sales, B. D. *Psychologists in competency to stand trial proceedings.* In preparation.
5. Shah, S. Personal communication, June 1982.

References

Adkins, J. C. An art? A science? Or luck? *Trial,* 1968–1969, *5,* 37–39.

Aitken, C. Psychosomatic approach to medical rehabilitation. *Psychotherapy and Psychosomatics,* 1979, *31,* 277–282.

American Psychological Association. *Standards for providers of psychological services.* Washington, D. C.: Author, 1977.

American Psychological Association. Ethical principles of psychologists. *American Psychologist,* 1981, *36,* 633–638.

American Psychological Association, Committee on Professional Standards. Specialty guidelines for the delivery of services. *American Psychologist,* 1981, *36,* 639–681.

American Psychological Association, American Education Research Association, & National Council on Measurement in Education. *Standards for educational and psychological tests.* Washington, D. C.: American Psychological Association, 1974.

Appleman, J. A. Selection of the jury. *Trial Lawyer's Guide,* 1968, *12,* 207–239.

Bersoff, D. N. Testing and the law. *American Psychologist,* 1981, *36,* 1047–1056.

Bodin, H. S. *Selecting a jury.* New York: Practicing Law Institute, 1954.

Bray, R. M., & Noble, A. M. Authoritarianism and decisions of mock juries: Evidence jury bias and group polarization. *Journal of Personality and Social Psychology,* 1978, *36,* 1424–1430.

---

our standards would also be undesirable in those cases where research demonstrates that the law is based on invalid assumptions. As the ethical principles go on to note:

d. As practitioners and researchers, psychologists act in accord with Association standards and guidelines related to practice and to the conduct of research with human beings and animals. In the ordinary course of events, psychologists adhere to relevant governmental laws and institutional regulations. When federal, state, provincial, organizational or institutional laws, regulations, or practices are in conflict with Association standards and guidelines, psychologists make known their commitment to Association standards and guidelines and, wherever possible, work toward a resolution of the conflict. Both practitioners and researchers are concerned with the development of such legal and quasi-legal regulations as best serve the public interest, and they work toward changing existing regulations that are not beneficial to the public interest.

Conversely a professional organization's standards can and should influence the development and application of the law. For example, Lerner (1978) argues that the Supreme Court is relying on the *Standards for Educational and Psychological Tests* (APA, AERA, & NCME, 1974) for answers to technical psychometric questions raised in the application of the law to testing controversies that come before the court. I unfortunately cannot shed light on whether the APA standards have influenced the development of the law, but they should. For example, the APA standards relating to professional behavior should guide policy makers in setting up and operating the nation's health care delivery systems.

Broeder, D. W. The voir dire examination—An empirical study. *Southern California Law Review,* 1965, *38*(4), 503–528.

Brunette, S. A., & Sales, B. D. The role of psychologists in state legislation governing sex offenders. *Professional Psychology,* 1980, *11,* 194–201.

Carroll, J. S., & Perlman, D. (Eds.). Attributions in the criminal justice system. Special issue of *Law and Human Behavior,* 1978, *2*(4), 285–401.

Comment. Academic researchers and the First Amendment: Constitutional protection for their confidential sources. *San Diego Law Review,* 1977, *14,* 876–903.

Darrow, C. Attorney for the defense. *Esquire Magazine,* May 1936, 36–37, 211–213.

Davis, B. E., & Wiley, R. E. Forty-nine thoughts on jury selection. *Trial Lawyer's Guide,* 1965, *9,* 351–356.

Dekraai, M. B., & Sales, B. D. Privileged communications of psychologists. *Professional Psychology,* 1982, *13,* 372–388.

DeLeon, P. H. The changing and creating of legislation: The political process. In B. D. Sales, *The professional psychologist's handbook.* New York: Plenum, 1983.

DeLeon, P. H., O'Keefe, A. M., VandenBos, G. R., & Kraut, A. G. How to influence public policy. *American Psychologist,* 1982, *37,* 476–485.

Diamond, S. (Ed.) *Simulation research and the law.* Special issue of *Law and Human Behavior,* 1979, *3*(1/2), 1–148.

Dix, G. E., & Poythress, N. G., Jr. Propriety of medical dominance of forensic mental health practice: The empirical evidence. *Arizona Law Review,* 1981, *23,* 961–989.

Dorken, H. Coming of age legislatively: In 21 steps. *American Psychologist,* 1981, *36,* 165–173.

Dorken, H. Health insurance and third-party reimbursement. In B. D. Sales (Ed.), *Professional psychologist's handbook.* New York: Plenum, 1983.

Education for All Handicapped Children Act, 20 U.S.C. § 1401 et seq, 1975.

Elwork, A., Sales, B. D., & Alfini, J. Juridic decisions: In ignorance of the law or in light of it? *Law and Human Behavior,* 1977, *1,* 163–189.

Elwork, A., Sales, B. D., & Alfini, J. *Making jury instructions understandable.* Charlottesville, Va.: Michie/Bobbs-Merrill, 1982.

Epstein, G. N., Steingarten, J., Weinstein, H. D., & Mashel, H. M. Panel report: Impact of law on the practice of psychotherapy. *Journal of Psychiatry and Law,* 1977, *5,* 7–40.

Feldman, S., & Wilson, K. The value of interpersonal skills in lawyering. *Law and Human Behavior,* 1981, *5,* 311–324.

Field, L. Voir dire examination—A neglected art. *University of Missouri at Kansas City Law Review,* 1965, *33,* 171–178.

Forman, B. D., & Shackar, S. A. Elevating the status of psychologists: A simple solution. *Professional Psychology,* 1981, *12,* 291–292.

Goldstein, I. *Trial technique.* Chicago: Callaghan, 1938.

Greenberg, M. S., & Ruback, R. B. *Social psychology and the criminal justice system.* Monterey, Calif.: Brooks/Cole, 1982.

Grisso, T. *Juveniles' waiver of rights: Legal and psychological competence.* New York: Plenum, 1981.

Harrington, D. C., & Dempsey, J. Psychological factors in jury selection. *Tennessee Law Review,* 1969, *37,* 173–184.

Hogan, D. *The regulation of psychotherapists* (4 vols.). Cambridge, Mass.: Balliner, 1979.

Katz, L. S. The twelve man jury. *Trial,* 1968–1969, *5,* 39–40, 42.

Kiesler, C. A. Mental health policy as a field of inquiry for psychology. *American Psychologist,* 1980, *35,* 1066–1080.

Knapp, S., & Vandecreek, L. Behavioral medicine: Its malpractice risks for psychologists. *Professional Psychology,* 1981, *12,* 677–683.

Knapp, S., & Vandecreek, L. Tarasoff: Five years later. *Professional Psychology,* 1982, *13,* 511–516.

Knerr, C. R., & Carroll, J. D. Confidentiality and criminal research: The evolving body of law. *Journal of Criminal Law and Criminology,* 1978, *69,* 311–321.

Konečni, V. J., & Ebbesen, E. B. Social-psychological approaches to legal issues. In B. D. Sales (Ed.), *The trial process.* New York: Plenum, 1981.

Konečni, V. J., & Ebbesen, E. B. *The criminal justice system: A social-psychological analysis.* San Francisco: W. H. Freeman, 1982.

Koocher, G. P. Ethical and professional standards in psychology. In B. D. Sales (Ed.), *Professional psychologist's handbook.* New York: Plenum, 1983.

Lerner, B. The Supreme Court and the APA, AERA, NCME test standards. *American Psychologist,* 1978, *33,* 915–919.

Lerner, B. The minimum competence testing movement: Social, scientific, and legal implications. *American Psychologist,* 1981, *36,* 1057–1066.

Levine, M. Scientific method and the adversarial model: Some preliminary thoughts. *American Psychologist,* 1974, *29,* 661–677.

Loftus, E. *Eyewitness testimony.* Cambridge: Harvard University Press, 1979.

Massad, P., Sales, B. D., & Acosta, E. Utilizing social science information in the policy process: Can psychologists help? In R. Kidd & M. Saks (Eds.), *Advances in applied social psychology. Vol. II.* Hillsdale, N. J.: Erlbaum, 1983.

Melton, G. B., Koocher, G. P., & Saks, M. J. *Children's competence to consent.* New York: Plenum, 1983.

Merrikin, K. H., Overcast, T. D., & Sales, B. D. Worker's compensation law and the compensability of mental injuries. *Health Psychology,* 1982, *1,* 373–387.

Meyer, R. G., & Smith, S. A crisis in group therapy. *American Psychologist,* 1977, *32,* 638–643.

Meyer, R. G., & Willage, D. E. Confidentiality and privileged communications in psychotherapy. In R. D. Lipsitt & B. D. Sales (Eds.), *New directions in psycholegal research.* New York: Van Nostrand Reinhold, 1980.

Monahan, J. *Predicting violent behavior and assessment of clinical techniques.* Beverly Hills, Calif.: Sage, 1981.

Morris, R., & Sales, B. D. Psychological testimony on the insanity defense. *American Psychologist,* in press.

Morris, R. A., Sales, B. D., & Berman, J. J. Research and the Freedom of Information Act. *American Psychologist,* 1981, *36,* 819–826.

Morse, S. J. Mental health law: Governmental regulation of disordered persons and the role of the professional psychologist. In B. D. Sales (Ed.), *Professional psychologist's handbook.* New York: Plenum, 1983.

Noll, J. O. The psychotherapist and informed consent. *American Journal of Psychiatry,* 1976, *133,* 1451–1453.

O'Connor v. Donaldson, 422 U.S. 563, 95 S.Ct. 2486 (1975).

Overcast, T. D., & Sales, B. D. Psychologists in state special education legislation. *Professional Psychology,* 1980, *11,* 775–783.

Overcast, T. D., & Sales, B. D. Psychological and multidisciplinary corporations. *Professional Psychology,* 1981, *12,* 749–760.

Overcast, T. D., & Sales, B. D. Elevating the status of psychologists: A simple solution is neither simple nor a solution. *Professional Psychology,* 1982, *13,* 171–172.

Poythress Jr., N. G. Psychiatric expertise in civil commitment: Training attorneys to cope with expert testimony. *Law and Human Behavior,* 1978, *2,* 1–24.

Roesch, R., & Golding, S. *Competency to stand trial.* Urbana: University of Illinois Press, 1980.

Rothblatt, H. B. Techniques for jury selection. *Criminal Law Bulletin,* 1966, *2*(4), 14–29.

Saks, M. J., & Hastie, R. *Social psychology in court.* New York: Van Nostrand Reinhold, 1978.

Sales, B. D. (Ed.). *The trial process.* New York: Plenum, 1981.

Sales, B. D., Overcast, T. D., & Merrikin, K. J. Worker's compensation protection for assaults and batteries on mental health professionals. In J. R. Lion & W. H. Reid (Eds.), *Assaults within psychiatric facilities.* New York: Grune & Stratton, in press.

Sales, B. D., Powell, D. M., Van Duizend, R. A., & Associates. *Disabled persons and the law: State legislative issues.* New York: Plenum, 1982.

Schaffer v. Spicer, 88 S.D. 36, 215 N.W.2d 134 (1974).

Schuchman, H. Confidentiality: Practice issues in new legislation. *American Journal of Orthopsychiatry,* 1980, *50,* 641–648.

Schwitzgebel, R. L., & Schwitzgebel, R. K. *Law and psychological practice.* New York: Wiley & Sons, 1980.

Shah, S. A. Dangerousness: A paradigm for exploring some issues in law and psychology. *American Psychologist,* 1978, *33,* 224–238.

Shah, S. A. Legal and mental health system interactions: Major developments and research needs. *International Journal of Law and Psychiatry,* 1981, *4,* 219–270.

Shepherd, J. C. Techniques of jury selection from the defendant's point of view. *Proceedings of the American Bar Association Section of Insurance, Negligence, and Compensation Law.* Chicago: American Bar Association, 1964–1965, 359–362.

Shuman, D. W., & Weiner, M. F. The privilege study: An empirical examination of the psychotherapist-patient privilege. *North Carolina Law Review,* 1982, *60,* 893–942.

Simon, G. C. Psychology, professional practice, and the public interest. In B. D. Sales (Ed.), *Professional psychologists handbook.* New York: Plenum, 1983.

Smith, D. Unfinished business with informed consent procedures. *American Psychologist,* 1981, *36,* 22–26.

Special Commission on the Social Sciences of the National Science Board. *Knowledge into action: Improving the nation's use of social sciences.* Washington, D. C.: National Science Foundation, 1969.

Stigall, T. T. Licensing and certification. In B. D. Sales (Ed.), *Professional psychologist's handbook.* New York: Plenum, 1983.

Tarasoff v. Board of Regents of University of California, 529 P.2d 553, 118 Cal. Rptr. 129 (1974), Vac. 17 Cal. 3d 425, 551 P.2d 334, 131 Cal. Rptr. 14 (1976).

Tate, E., Hawrish, E., & Clark, S. Communication variables in jury selection. *Journal of Communication,* 1974, *24,* 130–139.

Todd v. Goosetree, 493 S.W.2d 411 (1973 App.), *later app.* 528 S.W.2d 470.

Wells, G. (Ed.) *On eyewitness behavior.* Special issue of *Law and Human Behavior,* 1980, *4*(4), 237–394.

Wexler, D. B. Doctor-patient dialogue: A second opinion on talk therapy through law. *Yale Law Review,* 1980, *90,* 458–472.

Wexler, D. B. *Mental health law: The major issues.* New York: Plenum, 1981.

Woods, K. M., & McNamara, J. R. Confidentiality: Its effect on interviewer behavior. *Professional Psychology,* 1980, *11,* 714–721.

Zeisel, H., & Diamond, S. The effect of peremptory challenges on the jury and verdict. *Stanford Law Review,* 1978, *30,* 491–531.

DONALD N. BERSOFF

REGARDING PSYCHOLOGISTS TESTILY: THE LEGAL REGULATION OF PSYCHOLOGICAL ASSESSMENT

D onald N. Bersoff is a psychologist and a lawyer. In 1965 he obtained his doctorate from the School Psychology Program, New York University. He served as an Air Force psychologist, a teacher, a director of psychological services at Mansfield State College, a faculty member at Ohio State University with joint appointments in the Department of Psychology and on the Faculty for Exceptional Children, and an associate professor in the Department of Educational Psychology at the University of Georgia. He became increasingly concerned about the traditional use and interpretation of psychological tests and the restricted role of the school psychologist as a psychometric technician. Because he concluded that the practice of psychology was becoming increasingly legalized, Bersoff decided to combine his background in psychology with a legal career.

In 1976 Bersoff graduated from Yale Law School, where he served on the *Yale Law Journal.* He obtained a joint appointment as an assistant (then associate) professor at the University of Maryland School of Law and professor of psychology at Johns Hopkins University. In 1978 he founded an NIMH-funded JD–PhD program in law and psychology, a joint venture between Maryland and Hopkins, one of three of its kind in the country, for which he continues to serve as coordinator.

In late 1979 Bersoff became the first general counsel to the American Psychological Association (APA). Within two years what had begun as a part-time position became a full-time job within the law firm of Ennis, Friedman, Bersoff & Ewing, which represents APA.

Bersoff has been active in the American Psychological Association. He has served as president of the American Psychology-Law Society and has acted as a special consultant to a number of state departments of education and mental health facilities. In addition to litigation in the areas of psychological testing, special education, child advocacy, and the legal regulation of psychological practice, Bersoff has published several articles and chapters on these topics.

DONALD N. BERSOFF

REGARDING PSYCHOLOGISTS TESTILY: THE LEGAL REGULATION OF PSYCHOLOGICAL ASSESSMENT

S ince its beginning in World War I, the use of psychological tests has probably affected every person in the United States (Haney, 1981). Testing has become the means by which major decisions about people's lives are made in hospitals, mental health clinics, the military, the public civil service, private industry, and schools and colleges.

Tests, by and large, are neutral. Test scores have been used to admit, advance, and employ. For most people, however, test results have served as exclusionary mechanisms—to segregate, institutionalize, track, and deny access to coveted and increasingly scarce employment opportunities. As this use of tests increased, so did their potential for causing unjustified negative consequences. When those consequences led to legally cognizable injury, tests began to be examined by the legal system. As a result, probably no activity performed by psychologists is so closely scrutinized by the law.

This paper focuses on one particular injury—the claim that psychological tests are tools of discrimination that deny full realization of the rights of racial and ethnic minorities and of the handicapped. To make this presentation manageable, the discussion is limited to those two settings where the claim has been most pervasive: education and

Selected portions of this paper are based on material that has appeared elsewhere (Bersoff, 1979, 1981, 1982a, 1982b, in press).

employment. First, it may be helpful to understand the basic legal theories that permit the legal system to inquire about what is fundamentally a scientific and professional activity.

Legal Underpinnings

Although criticism of testing from social, political, and psychological commentators dates from 1922 (e.g., Amrine, 1965; Bersoff, 1973; Black, 1963; Cronbach, 1975; Gross, 1962; Hoffman, 1962; Kamin, 1974; Lippman, 1922; Williams, 1970), only in the last 15 years have legal scholars, the legislature, and the courts begun to examine their use. The recent activity, in turn, has generated intense reexamination by behavioral scientists. The American Psychological Association (APA) devoted an entire issue of the *American Psychologist* (Glaser & Bond, 1981) and a full day at its 1981 convention to testing; the National Academy of Sciences financed three extended examinations of the topic by blue-ribbon committees (Heller, Holtzman, & Messick, 1982; Sherman & Robinson, 1982; Wigdor & Garner, 1982). A joint committee of APA, American Educational Research Association (AERA), and National Council on Measurement in Education (NCME) began revising the *Standards of Psychological and Educational Tests* (1974), to be published in 1984.

The courts are traditionally wary of interfering with the discretion of trained experts, especially in those areas in which they concede a lack of specialized knowledge. Few fields of endeavor are more arcane and unknowable than measurement and evaluation. However, when the activities of psychologists directly and sharply impinge on fundamental values protected by the Constitution, the courts, as ultimate interpreters of its content, have found it appropriate to intervene.

Two basic constitutional values relevant to those who construct, use, interpret, and take tests appear in the fifth and fourteenth amendments. Generally those amendments serve as barriers to thoughtless and arbitrary actions by local, county, state, and federal officials (the Fifth Amendment pertains to the federal government; the Fourteenth to other governmental entities). The two most important concepts in those amendments are equal protection and due process. Under the Equal Protection Clause, governments are forbidden to treat differently persons who are similarly situated unless there is a supportable reason for so doing. When special groups of persons are affected by a state's action, the courts will scrutinize that action even more closely. For example, although the battle for the Equal Rights Amendment has been lost (at least for the time being), the Supreme Court has held that governmental bodies must produce substantial and legitimate reasons for detrimental gender-based actions. With regard to racial and ethnic minorities, the test is even more difficult. When a state has deliberately acted to the disadvantage of one of those groups, it must prove a compelling or overriding need to do so. Such proof is needed because these groups have been "saddled with such disabilities or . . . subjected to such a history of purposeful unequal treatment, or relegated to such a position of political powerlessness as to command extraordinary protection from the majoritarian political process" (*San Antonio Independent School District v. Rodriguez*, 1973, p. 28). The result, when courts apply this strict scrutiny test, is almost always against the government.

The Due Process Clause forbids the government from denying persons life, liberty, or property without a legitimate reason and without providing some meaningful and impartial forum to prevent arbitrary deprivations of those protected interests. Both property and liberty interests have been broadly defined by the Supreme Court. Property interests include any government-created entitlements such as tenure, licensure to practice one's profession, or access to public education. Liberty includes not only freedom from involuntary incarceration in a prison or commitment to a mental institution; it can also encompass the right to privacy, personal security, and reputation. For example, the Constitution prevents governmental institutions from unilateral, unsupportable, and stigmatizing labeling—official branding was what Justice Douglas once called it—of persons as handicapped or mentally ill. The procedures that due process may require under any given set of circumstances begin with a determination of the precise nature of the government function as well as the potential entitlement that will be lost as the result of the governmental action. Although the precise contours of due process change with the nature of the interest at stake, at bottom the clause requires fundamental fairness when the government deals with persons within its jurisdiction.

In addition to these constitutional guarantees, a whole litany of federal and state statutory protections may be invoked to challenge the inappropriate use of tests not only in the public sector but in private industry as well. Together, these enactments provide extensive armamentaria for potential plaintiffs.

With this background, let us now turn to some of the most important examples of challenges to tests in education and employment.

Education

Early History

The Supreme Court's ringing declarations in *Brown v. Board of Education* (1954) ended state-imposed segregation in the public schools. But in the decade after *Brown,* many southern school systems refused to accept the Court's decision as final. They interpreted the Court's assertion that separation of black children from white "solely because of their race generates a feeling of inferiority . . . that may affect their hearts and minds in a way unlikely ever to be undone" (p. 494) as an empirically testable hypothesis, not a normative legal principle. In the early 1960s, one of Georgia's school systems sought to disprove what it believed to be an erroneous factual premise. It attempted to show that differences in learning rates, cognitive ability, behavioral traits, and capacity for education in general were so great that not only was it impossible for black children and white children to be educated effectively in the same room but that to "congregate children of such diverse traits in schools . . . would seriously impair the educational opportunities of both white and Negro and cause them grave psychological harm" (*Stell v. Savannah-Chatham County Board of Education*, 1963, p. 668).

To prove their contentions the defendants called several expert witnesses, including two psychologists, Travis Osborne and Henry Garrett. Based on such instruments as the California Achievement Test and the California Mental Maturity Tests, Osborne and Garrett testified that significant differences in test scores were indicative of inherent differences in the races and that only minor changes could be achieved by educational readjustment or other environmental change. Although the test results that led these witnesses to conclude that black children were genetically inferior and the tests on which those conclusions were based went unchallenged by attorneys fighting to enforce desegregation, the idea that such devices could measure innate ability found its way into a 1967 decision that, at the time, became the most persuasive and widely quoted legal opinion of its kind. That case is *Hobson v. Hansen* (1967).

At issue in *Hobson* was not psychological testing but rather the constitutionality of disparities in the allocation of financial and educational resources in the Washington, D.C., public school system, which was charged with favoring white children. Also at issue was the overrepresentation of black children in lower, and white children in upper, ability groups. During the trial, however, it was adduced that the method by which track assignments were made depended almost entirely on such standardized group ability scales as the Metropolitan Readiness and Achievement Test and the Otis Quick-Scoring Mental Ability Test. Disproportional placement in programs was found to have a negative impact on black children; such placement, determined primarily by reliance on standardized tests, triggered the court's intensive inquiry into the nature and limitations of standardized tests.

The court decided that classification on the basis of ability could be defended only if such judgments were based on measures that assessed children's capacity to learn, i.e., their innate endowment, not their skill levels. The court concluded that the assessment devices on which the classifications depend did not accurately reflect students' learning abil-

REGULATION OF PSYCHOLOGICAL ASSESSMENT

ity. The inevitable result was that ability grouping and the group tests relied on for tracking decisions were ruled unconstitutional. The words that the court used to condemn the school system's practices were to have a profound effect on the use of psychological tests during the next decade.

> The evidence shows that the method by which track assignments are made depends essentially on standardized aptitude tests which, although given on a system-wide basis, are completely inappropriate for use with a large segment of the student body. Because these tests are standardized primarily on and are relevant to a white middle class group of students, they produce inaccurate and misleading test scores when given to lower class and Negro students . . . [T]hese students are in reality being classified . . . [on] factors which have nothing to do with innate ability. (*Hobson v. Hansen*, 1967, p. 514)

When read in its entirety, *Hobson* represents the justified condemnation of rigid, poorly conceived classification practices that negatively affected the educational opportunities of minority children and led to permanent stigmatization of blacks as unteachable. But swept within *Hobson*'s condemnation of harmful classification practices were ability tests used as the sole or primary decision-making devices to justify placement. Tests were banned unless they could be shown to measure children's innate capacity to learn. No psychologist who has written on the subject, including Jensen (1969, 1980), believes that tests measure hereditary endowment solely (e.g., Anastasi, 1976; Cleary, Humphreys, Kendrick, & Wesman, 1975). If that were the criterion, no test could pass it.

The decision, however, stimulated a round of post-*Hobson* cases throughout the country. In many southern school systems during the early 1970s, any kind of ability or achievement testing for purposes of pupil assignment was banned until unitary school systems were established. In the Southwest another group of cases had two new significant dimensions. First, the plaintiffs were Hispanics, rather than blacks. Second, the cases that they brought began to attack the stately, revered, and venerated devices against which all other tests were measured: the individual intelligence scales such as the Stanford-Binet and the Wechsler Intelligence Scale for Children (WISC). The most important trio of cases, *Covarrubias v. San Diego Unified School District* (1971), *Guadalupe Organization, Inc. v. Tempe School District No. 3* (1971), and *Diana v. State Board of Education* (1970) were settled out of court by consent decree, but each led to important changes in school testing policy that foretold more pervasive developments.

Individual Intelligence Tests: Larry P. v. Riles

The decade from 1971 to 1980 brought the most severe challenge to the use of individual intelligence scales as the result of federal court decisions in San Francisco, *Larry P. v. Riles* (1979), and Chicago, *PASE (Parents in Action on Special Education) v. Hannon* (1980). If *Hobson* is the seminal case of the 1960s, *Larry P. v. Riles* (1972, 1979) deserves similar status for the 1970s. The trial court's decision on the merits, which took eight years to reach, threatens the continued administration of individual intelligence tests and the existence of educable mentally retarded (EMR) classes as they pertain to minority children. As the rationale of the decision will almost certainly guide litigation concerning psychological assessment, the case warrants detailed examination. The case has had two phases: the grant of a preliminary injunction in 1972 (*Riles I*) and the decision on the merits in 1979 (*Riles II*).

In 1971 black children attending the San Francisco schools filed suit, charging discrimination and misplacement in EMR classes as a result of the administration of state-approved intelligence tests. The plaintiffs claimed that they were not mentally retarded and that the tests used to place them were culturally biased. They requested that the court grant a preliminary injunction restraining the school system from administering IQ tests to determine EMR placement of black children until a full trial could decide the merits of their complaint.

In 1971 the legal importance of the case lay in the plaintiff's contention that the testing practices in San Francisco resulted in a disproportionate and harmful impact on black children in violation of the Equal Protection Clause. Framed in that manner, a court was faced squarely for the first time with the issue of the constitutionality of individual psychological testing when used for placement in classes for the retarded in situations adversely affecting racial minorities.

Although blacks constituted 28.5 percent of students in the San Francisco school system, 66 percent of all students in its EMR program were black. Similarly, although blacks comprised 9.1 percent of the California school population, 27 percent of all school children in the state's EMR classes were black. Thus the plaintiffs contended that, although placement in EMR classes was based on intelligence, not race, the method of classification led to a disproportionate impact on black children.

The year before *Larry P.* was first heard, the Supreme Court had decided *Griggs v. Duke Power Co.* (1971). In an action brought under Title VII of the 1964 Civil Rights Act, black employees challenged the use of intelligence tests as a condition of employment or transfer to certain positions for which they were otherwise qualified. The employers claimed that, although the use of the test may have had a discriminatory effect in that fewer blacks were hired or promoted, there was no intent to discriminate. The Supreme Court, however, interpreted the Civil

Rights Act as proscribing "not only overt discrimination but also practices that are fair in form, but discriminatory in operation" (*Griggs v. Duke Power Co.*, 1971, p. 431). It declared that "good intent or absence of discriminatory intent does not redeem . . . testing mechanisms that operate as 'built-in headwinds' for minority groups . . . " (p. 432). Once the discriminatory effect was shown, the Court placed the burden in cases brought under the Civil Rights Act on defendants to show "that any given requirement ha[d] a manifest relationship to the employment in question" (p. 432).

Faced with the task of demonstrating a rational connection between the IQ tests and their use, i.e., placement in EMR classes, San Francisco in 1972 conceded that the tests were racially and culturally biased but justified continued use because, in the absence of suitable alternatives, the tests were the best means available for the purpose of classifying students as retarded. The court retorted that "the absence of any rational means of identifying children in need of such treatment can hardly render acceptable an otherwise concededly irrational means, such as the IQ tests as it is presently administered to black students" (*Riles I*, 1972, p. 1313).

Other attempts to sustain the reasonableness of their practices or to explain racial disproportionality in EMR programs were rejected; the school system's practices were adjudged to violate the Equal Protection Clause. The court enjoined placement of black children in EMR classes on the basis of criteria that relied primarily on the results of intelligence tests and led to racial imbalance in such classes (for an empirically based defense of the part that school psychologists played in the evaluation of these children, see Meyers, Macmillan, & Yoshida, 1978).

After the 1972 decision. Three events followed. An appellate tribunal in 1974 affirmed the lower court's order holding that "the carefully limited relief granted [was] justified by the 'peculiar facts' in this case" (*Larry P. v. Riles*, 1974, p. 965). Then the trial court approved the plaintiff's motion to broaden the injunction to prohibit the administration of individual intelligence tests to all black children in the state. Finally, California decided to go beyond even that ban. In 1975 it issued a resolution that, until further notice, none of the IQ tests on its approved list could be used to place any children regardless of race in EMR classes.

This activity ended the first phase of the case. The second phase, the trial on the substantive issues, lasted from October 1977 through mid-1978, producing over 10,000 pages of testimony. Finally in October 1979 the court published its opinion, in which it decided whether the preliminary injunction that it granted in 1972 should become permanent.

Three elements in *Riles I* assumed importance as a result of subsequent actions by the Supreme Court and Congress. First, the plaintiffs claimed that the defendants had infringed constitutional rights, not that they had violated a federal or state statute. Second, the court ruled that injury resulted only from an intelligence classification that had a discriminatory effect, not from an intent to discriminate. Third, the court had relied heavily on *Griggs v. Duke Power Co.* (1971) to support its decision that the defendant had the burden of persuasion concerning the reasonableness of its testing practices. Each element was eventually to cause serious problems for the plaintiffs as a result of legal activity between 1972 and 1979.

Of crucial importance was the Supreme Court's decision in 1976 in *Washington v. Davis*, an employment discrimination case that has had a significant impact on testing litigation brought on grounds similar to that in *Larry P.* In a decision that surprised and angered many civil rights advocates, the Supreme Court rejected the contention that the *constitutional* standard for adjudicating claims of racial discrimination was identical to the *statutory* standard under Title VII of the Civil Rights Act: "[O]ur cases have not embraced the proposition that a law or other official act, without regard to whether it reflects a racially discriminatory purpose, is unconstitutional *solely* because it has a racially disproportionate impact" (*Washington v. Davis*, 1976, p. 239). Thus the Court declined to apply the more rigorous standard of the Civil Rights Act to the Constitution. Since 1976 the Supreme Court has made it clear that disproportionate impact

> is not the sole touchstone of an invidious racial discrimination forbidden by the Constitution. Standing alone, it does not trigger the rule . . . that racial classifications are to be subjected to the strictest scrutiny and are justifiable only by the weightiest of considerations. (*Washington v. Davis*, 1976, p. 237)

Davis severely undercut the chances of the plaintiffs in *Riles* to gain eventual victory on the merits. Given that when a constitutional injury is alleged, minority plaintiffs must prove intent to discriminate, the *Riles* court could hardly employ the same reasoning that was persuasive at the preliminary injunction stage. To find a constitutional violation in *Riles II*, the court would have to sift through the testimony to uncover evidence of discriminatory intent, not merely of discriminatory effect. This increased the burden on the plaintiffs; proving discrimination is more difficult when intent rather than effect (i.e., statistical disparity) is at issue.

Significantly, while the Supreme Court was restricting the reach of the Equal Protection Clause, Congress enacted a series of laws that continue to have a considerable impact on the practice of psychological assessment in the public schools. In 1975 Congress passed Public Law 94–142 (20 U.S.C. §§1401–1461), the Education for All Handicapped Children Act, extending the legislation protecting handicapped students first passed in 1966 and 1974. Two years earlier it enacted Section 504 of the Rehabilitation Act of 1973 (29 U.S.C. §794) and subsequently amended it in 1978. Implementing regulations for both those bills were drafted by the Department of Health, Education, and Welfare (DHEW—now Department of Health and Human Services and the Department of Education), which took effect in 1977.

Public Law 94–142 is essentially a statute providing financial support to state and local education agencies for special education and related services if the agencies meet certain detailed eligibility requirements. Earlier legislation (Pub. L. 93–380) had put school systems on notice that they would have to develop methods for ensuring that any assessment devices used "for the purposes of classification and placement of handicapped children will be selected and administered so as not to be racially and culturally discriminatory." Public Law 94–142 and its implementing regulations reaffirmed this mandate concerning nondiscriminatory evaluation and fleshed out the meaning of this requirement:

> (a) Tests and other evaluation materials:
> (1) Are provided and administered in the child's native language or other mode of communication . . . .
> (2) Have been validated for the specific purpose for which they are used; and
> (3) Are administered by trained personnel in conformance with instructions provided by their provider . . . .
> (34 C.F.R. § 300.532)

The most ambiguous of these provisions is (a) (2). The regulations, on their face, require test validation but not test validity. Even if one infers that both are necessary, there is no indication to what level of validity a test must conform. Validity coefficients that psychologists find acceptable may not pass constitutional muster. One court has ruled that "when a program talks about labeling someone as a particular type and such a label could remain with him for the remainder of his life, the margin of error must be almost nil" (*Merriken v. Cressman*, 1973, p. 920). *Nil* implies almost perfect coefficients. Few, if any, psychometric instruments yield reliability, much less validity, coefficients above .95. Until the decision in *Riles II*, there were few clearcut judicial or statutory guidelines with regard to standards of validity in school testing or the general concept of nondiscriminatory assessment (see Neuberger, 1981; Smith, 1980).

With regard to the 1973 rehabilitation act, a multipurpose law to promote the education, employment, and training of handicapped persons, Congress declared in Section 504: "No otherwise qualified handicapped individual in the United States . . . shall, solely by reason of his handicap, be excluded from participation in, be denied the benefits of, or be subjected to discrimination under any program or activity receiving federal financial assistance." This section represents the first federal

---

civil rights law protecting the rights of handicapped persons and reflects a national commitment to end discrimination on the basis of handicap. Unlike Public Law 94–142, the requirements of Section 504 are not triggered by receipt of funds under a specific statute but protect handicapped persons in all institutions receiving federal financial assistance. Any school system, public or private, receiving federal monies for any program or activity whatsoever, is bound by its mandates.

In mid-1977 the Office of Civil Rights, DHEW, published a lengthy set of regulations implementing the broad right-granting language of Section 504. Subpart D pertains to preschool, elementary, and secondary education. In addition to general principles already established under Public Law 94–142, the regulations include rules for the evaluation of children suspected of being handicapped. The language of those provisions (including the requirement of validated tests) are almost identical to that in the implementing regulations to Public Law 94–142; they will not be repeated here (see 34 C.F.R. § 104.35).

Given the outcome in *Washington v. Davis* (1976) and the passage of federal legislation protecting handicapped persons, the plaintiffs in *Larry P.* sought to amend their original complaint in an attempt to increase their chances of eventual victory. In 1977 they filed an amendment alleging, in addition to the equal protection claim under the Constitution, that the defendants had violated the 1964 Civil Rights Act (with that, the court presumed, only discriminatory effect, not intent, would have to be proved). The court granted the motion to amend. Later that year it also granted a motion permitting the U.S. Department of Justice to participate as amicus curiae. The government, siding with the plaintiffs, asserted that the state's conduct also violated Public Law 94–142 and Section 504. The plaintiffs then filed a motion asking to amend its complaint a second time in order to include an allegation that the defendants violated Public Law 94–142. This motion was granted.

The 1979 decision. Judge Peckham finally published his long, controversial opinion on the merits in October 1979. The court found in favor of the plaintiffs on both statutory and constitutional grounds. It permanently enjoined the defendants "from utilizing, permitting the use of, or approving the use of any standardized tests . . . for the identification of black EMR children or their placement into EMR classes, without first securing prior approval by this court" (p. 989).

The court's primary focus was on the nondiscriminatory provisions of Section 504 and Public Law 94–142, particularly the implementing regulations requiring that the assessment instruments be "validated for the specific purpose for which they are used." The court's interpretation of these provisions—of crucial importance in its ultimate decision and the shaping of the final remedy—broke new ground, for, as the court recognized, "there are no cases applying validation criteria to tests used for EMR placement" (p. 969).

The court held that defendants should bear the burden of proving that the tests used for placement had been validated for black children. However, it would not accept proof merely that the tests could be used to predict school performance. It adopted the more stringent requirement that the tests be shown valid for selecting children who would be unable to profit from instruction in regular classes with remedial instruction. The tests would have to identify accurately those children who belonged in what the court characterized as isolated, dead-end, stigmatizing EMR programs. This kind of validation, the court found, had not been done. "[D]efendants must come forward and show that they [the tests] have been validated for each minority group with which they are used. . . . This minimal burden has not been met for diagnosing the kind of mental retardation justifying the EMR placement" (p. 971).

The court rejected validity studies correlating IQ scores with college grades or with other achievement tests. It was satisfied only with research relating IQ scores for black children with classroom grades, although the latter were admittedly subjective. The one relevant study cited (Goldman & Hartig, 1976) yielded correlations between IQ scores and grades for white children of .25 and only .14 for blacks. On that basis one prominent psychologist testified that the WISC had "little or no validity for predicting the scholastic performance of black or brown children" (p. 972). (For a methodological critique of this study, see Messé, Crano, Messé, & Rice, 1979.) Thus the court concluded that "the I.Q. tests are differentially valid for black and white children. . . . Differential validity means that more errors will be made for black children than whites, and that is unacceptable" (p. 973).

The court continued its analysis and found that alternative mechanisms for determining placement in EMR classes did exist. Between 1975 and the resolution of this case in 1979, there had been a statewide moratorium on the use of IQ tests to place all children, regardless of race, in EMR programs. The state's own employees, called as adverse witnesses by the plaintiffs, testified that adequate assessments had been made during that period without IQ tests and that no evidence suggested that misplacements had occurred. The court found that more time and care had been taken during this period in placing children in EMR classes. Nevertheless, the court warned, alternatives to IQ tests had not been validated, and disproportionate placement, while less egregious than in the pre-1975 era, still existed. Continued use of tests would still be needed, not, however, for the purpose of labeling children as retarded but for "the development of curricula that respond to specific educational needs" (p. 974).

Judge Peckham was not content to rest his decision solely on statutory grounds. Testing for EMR placement had been preliminarily enjoined in *Riles I* on the basis of equal protection claims, and the court felt bound to determine whether the plaintiffs continued to warrant relief under the Constitution "where this litigation commenced" (p. 975). But the plaintiffs' task under the Fourteenth Amendment, given *Davis*, was not as simple as under federal law. "The difficult question of intent [had] moved to center stage" (p. 975). The court felt compelled to go beyond equating disproportionate impact with discriminatory intent, although that impact might have been the natural and foreseeable result of the state's conduct. The plaintiffs had to prove more. In *Riles II* the court made clear that it would not so narrowly define discriminatory purpose "to mean an intent to harm black children"(p. 979). It would suffice if plaintiffs showed an intent to segregate those children into classes for the educably retarded. In the end the court was satisfied that the plaintiffs had met this burden.

The EMR program received the brunt of the court's condemnation. Throughout the opinion Judge Peckham labeled the program "dead-end," "isolating," "inferior," and "stigmatizing." The court concluded that EMR classes were "designed to separate out children who are *incapable* of learning in regular classes" (p. 941, emphasis in the original) and such classes were not meant to provide remedial instruction so that children could learn the skills necessary for eventual return to regular instruction. Given these characteristics, the court considered "the decision to place children in these classes . . . a crucial one. Children wrongly placed in these classes are unlikely to escape as they inevitably lag farther and farther behind the children in regular classes" (p. 942). Coupled with this pejorative view of the EMR program was the undeniable, substantial overrepresentation of black children in those classes, a fact essentially unchanged from *Riles I*.

The next step in the court's analysis was a review of the process by which a disproportionate number of black children were placed in EMR classes. The court found that, although California had acknowledged in 1969 that minorities were overrepresented in EMR classes, the state chose that year for the first time to mandate the use of specific standardized individual intelligence tests for EMR placement. The list had been developed by a state department of education official who was not an expert in IQ testing, it had been formulated primarily by surveying the tests most frequently used by California's school psychologists and be relying on the recommendations of test publishers. The court concluded that this "quick and unsystematic" process failed to consider "critical issues stemming from IQ testing" (p. 946), and its reaction was harsh: "[B]y relying on the most commonly used tests, they [the defendants] opted to perpetuate any discriminatory effects of those tests" (p. 947).

The court also found that despite California's statutory scheme requiring the consideration of other pertinent and specified data, "the I.Q. score was clearly the most scrupulously kept record, and it appears to have been the most important one" (p. 950). Thus the court hypothesized, "if the I.Q. tests are discriminatory, they inevitably must bias the entire process" (p. 950).

These initial analyses brought the court to the central issue: the nature of the intelligence tests. Expert witnesses for both plaintiffs and defendants agreed on two crucial facts. First, it was impossible to "truly define, much less measure, intelligence;" instead, "I.Q. tests, like other ability tests, essentially measure achievement . . . " (p. 38). This finding was a significant departure from the assumption in *Hobson* and *Riles I* that the tests measure innate ability. Second, black children did significantly less well on intelligence tests than their white counterparts. Only 2 percent of white students in California achieved IQ scores below 70 while 15 percent of black students did. The court then proceeded to determine if there were any acceptable explanations for the significantly disparate scores of blacks and whites on IQ tests.

It confronted the most controversial explanation first—that the differences between the races were genetic in origin—but rejected any notion of inherent inferiority in black children. The defendants themselves eschewed reliance on this ground, although at least one psychological expert witness for the state did not rule out such an explanation. The court reasoned that the genetic theory overlooked the possibility of bias in the tests and noted that believing intelligence is inherited did not lead inexorably to the conclusion that blacks were intellectually inferior.

The court gave somewhat more serious consideration to a socioeconomic theory on which the defendants relied. The state claimed that differences in scores resulted from the rearing of poor children, both black and white, in inadequate homes and neighborhoods. Although the court could accept the theory that poverty resulted in mental retardation, it refused to conclude that membership in the lower socioeconomic classes produced substantially more mentally retarded children.

The court then examined the hypothesis that cultural bias in the tests was the most cogent explanation for the disparities. The court noted that versions of the Stanford-Binet and Wechsler scales before the 1970s had been developed with only white children used in the process of deriving norms against which all children would be measured. That these tests had been restandardized in the early 1970s to include a representative proportion of black children did not satisfy the court that they were valid for culturally different groups. "Mixing the populations without more does not eliminate any preexisting bias" (p. 957). The process failed to yield data that could be used to compare black and white children's performance on particular items.

The court identified two other indexes of cultural bias. First, to the extent that black children were more likely to be exposed to nonstandard English, they would be handicapped in the verbal component of intelligence tests. Second, certain items regarding the scoring criteria were inherently unfair to black children from culturally different environments. The court concluded that "to the extent that a 'black culture' exists and translates the phenomenon of intelligence into skills and knowledge untested by the standardized intelligence tests, those tests cannot measure the capabilities of black children" (p. 960). The court charged that the tests were never designed to eliminate bias against black children and blamed test developers and users for assuming "in effect that black children were less 'intelligent' than whites" (pp. 956–957).

Thus the plaintiffs were held to have proved discriminatory intent. The defendants could prevail only if explanations for their conduct passed muster under the most exacting of the equal protection tests. However, the court held that "defendants can establish no compelling state interest in the use of the I.Q. tests nor in the maintenance of EMR classes with overwhelming disproportions of black enrollment" (p. 985).

After finding for the plaintiffs under both federal law and the Constitution (as well as the California Constitution), the court had to forge proper remedies. It recognized the genuine changes initiated by California during the litigation and the complexity and risk of judicial interference in the administration of education. The court did not want its condemnation of intelligence tests seen as the final judgment on the scientific validity of such devices. But these concerns did not dissuade the court from holding the state responsible for its failure to assess and educate black children properly and from fashioning remedies to halt both test abuse and disproportionate enrollment of blacks in EMR classes.

The court permanently enjoined the state from using any standardized intelligence tests to identify black children for EMR placement without first securing court approval. The state board of education would have to petition the court after determining that the tests were not racially or culturally discriminatory, that they would be administered in a nondiscriminatory manner, and that they had been validated for the purpose of placing black children in EMR classes. The petition would have to be supported by statistical evidence submitted under oath and by certification that public hearings had been held on the proposed tests.

With regard to disproportionate placement, the state was ordered to monitor and eliminate overrepresentation of black students by obtaining annual data documenting enrollment in EMR classes by race and ethnicity and by requiring each school district to prepare and adopt plans to correct significant imbalances. To remedy the harm to children who had been misidentified, the defendants were to reevaluate all black children labeled as educably retarded with only standardized intelligence tests approved by the court. Finally, schools would have to draft individual education plans designed to return all incorrectly identified children to regular classrooms.

The decision, over the objection of the California State Board of Education, has been appealed by Defendant Riles to the Ninth Circuit Court of Appeals. The appellate tribunal heard the case in November 1981, but the decision is not expected until late 1983.

PASE v. Hannon. Almost nine months to the day after Judge Peckham issued his opinion in *Riles II*, Judge Grady, a federal court judge in Illinois, rendered his decision in *PASE v. Hannon* (1980). Although the facts, issues, claims, and witnesses were similar to *Larry P.*, the analysis and outcome could not have been more different. Rather than ruling that the tests in question were culturally biased, as Judge Peckham did, Judge Grady held

> that the WISC, WISC-R and Stanford-Binet tests, when used in conjunction with the statutorily mandated [other criteria] for determining an appropriate educational program for a child [under Pub. L. 94–142] . . . do not discriminate against black children in the Chicago public schools. Defendants are complying with the statutory mandate. (*PASE v. Hannon*, 1980, p. 883)

The case was brought on behalf of all black children who were or would be placed in Chicago's EMR classes. As in *Larry P.* the plaintiffs claimed that blacks were overrepresented in those programs. As in San Francisco, Chicago's EMR curriculum is limited to helping the child become economically independent. Children who graduate from EMR classes are not qualified for college entrance, nor do they receive a regular diploma. The court called inappropriate placement in EMR classes "an educational tragedy" (p. 834) and accepted as fact that, even for children properly placed, EMR students "suffer from feelings of inferiority" (p. 834).

Using a strategy similar to that in *Larry P.*, the two named plaintiffs in *PASE* showed that, although they were placed in EMR classes for several years, they were not genuinely retarded. Reevaluations indicated that they were children of normal intelligence whose learning was hampered by remediable disabilities. The plaintiffs claimed that the misassessment was caused by racial bias in the individually administered IQ tests. The use of those tests, they claimed, violated the Equal Protection Clause of the Constitution, as well as the same federal statutes at issue in *Larry P.* Unlike *Larry P.* this trial lasted only three weeks. Many of the witnesses who appeared in *Riles II* also testified for the plaintiffs in *PASE* and offered similar testimony concerning the history of IQ misuse and cultural bias. The defendants conceded that the tests could be slightly biased but asserted that this did not deprive the tests of their utility, nor did the use of the tests result in misclassification. The school system reminded the court that the ultimate diagnosis of retardation was based on a combination of factors and that the IQ score was only one of them. School officials were concerned that the absence of this relatively objective measure would force a school to make decisions on predominantly subjective criteria.

Whereas Judge Peckham carefully listened to the opinions of the expert witnesses who testified in San Francisco and frequently cited them, Judge Grady was significantly less influenced by those same witnesses in Chicago.

> None of the witnesses in this case has so impressed me with his or her credibility or expertise that I would feel secure in basing a decision simply upon his or her opinion. In some instances, I am satisfied that the opinions expressed are more the result of doctrinaire commitment to a preconceived idea than they are the result of scientific inquiry. I need something more than the conclusions of the witnesses in order to arrive at my own conclusion. (p. 836)

Judge Grady stated that he had considered the expert testimony but was not bound by it. What he felt imperative was to examine the tests item by item, so that he could judge for himself whether the claim of cultural bias could be sustained. He concluded that an informed decision concerning the question could not be reached in any other way. He had no reservations about his competence to make those determinations. Thus, in a startling and extraordinary maneuver, Judge Grady proceeded to cite every question on the WISC, WISC-R, and the Stanford-Binet tests and to give every acceptable response in order to determine which items were culturally biased against black children. This process took nearly 35 pages of the court's 52-page opinion.

The court's conclusion. The end result of this analysis was the court's conclusion that only eight items on the WISC or WISC-R and one item on the Binet were "biased or so subject to suspicion of bias that they should not be used" (p. 875). Judge Grady rejected the assertions of Robert Williams, the black psychologist who had devised the BITCH test (Black Intelligence Test of Cultural Homogeneity), that many other items were unfair to blacks.

> It would be possible to devise countless esoteric tests which would be failed by persons unfamiliar with particular subject matter. Every ethnic group . . . has its own vocabulary, its own universe of information, which is not generally shared by others. The fact that it would be possible to prepare an unfair test does not prove that the Wechsler or Stanford-Binet tests are unfair.
>
> Dr. Williams' criticism of many test items appear unrelated to the question of racial bias. In fact, of the relatively few items he did discuss, most of them were criticized as inappropriate tests of any child's intelligence, not simply a black child's intelligence. (pp. 874–875)

If the tests were not culturally biased, what was the explanation for the significant mean differences between white and black children's IQ scores? Like the parties in *Larry P.*, both the plaintiffs and defendants in

PASE rejected a genetic theory: "There is no dispute . . . about the equality of innate intellectual capacity. Defendants assert no less strongly than plaintiffs that there are no genetic differences in mental capacity" (p. 877). Unlike the court in both *Riles I & II*, where Judge Peckham had rejected a socioeconomic explanation, Judge Grady found that argument persuasive. Accepting the arguments of the school system's witnesses that the acquisition of intellectual skills is greatly affected by a child's early intellectual stimulation, the court reasoned:

> Defendant's explanation of the I.Q. difference, that it is caused by socio-economic factors . . . is consistent with other circumstances not accounted for by plaintiff's theory of cultural bias. It is uncontradicted that most of the children in the EMH classes do in fact come from the poverty pockets of the city. This tends to suggest that what is involved in not simply race but something associated with poverty. It is also significant that many black children who take the test score at levels high enough to preclude EMR placement. Plaintiffs have not explained why the alleged cultural bias of the tests did not result in EMH level scores for these children. Plaintiffs' theory of cultural bias simply ignores the fact that black children perform differently from each other on the tests. It also fails to explain the fact that some black children perform better than most whites. (p. 878)

The court concluded that the plaintiffs had failed to prove their contention that the intelligence tests were culturally unfair to black children. Even if they were, the court believed that such unfairness would not make the assessment process biased. Judge Grady read Public Law 94–142's prohibition against single measures and its requirement of nondiscriminatory assessment as meaning that the entire psychoeducational evaluation, when viewed as a whole, had to be nonbiased. A single procedure by itself could be discriminatory without condemning as invalid the entire system for placing minority children in EMR programs. The court reasoned that multiple procedures ensured that results from the intelligence test would be interpreted in the light of other evaluation devices and information sources.

The court in *PASE,* therefore, viewed the placement process as a protective device against misclassification, in contrast to the court in *Riles II,* which concentrated on an analysis of the tests. Judge Peckham found California's system of assessment sound in theory but condemned it in practice, finding that testing continued to be the most important determinant of EMR placement. Judge Grady scrutinized the process in Chicago and concluded that referral, screening, multidisciplinary evaluation, and the staff conference helped prevent misclassification. He found that for all subranges within the EMR classification scheme fewer children were ultimately labeled retarded than would have been the case based on their IQ score alone. Although the court conceded that some children were misplaced, it rejected the hypothesis that erroneous placements were due to racial bias in the intelligence tests. (However, for research that casts serious doubt on this analysis and concludes that IQ is the critical causal variable in the placement, see Berk, Bridges, & Shih, 1981.)

What bearing did Judge Peckham's decision in *Riles II* have? Judge Grady's reference to *Larry P.* occupied a bit less than one page of his long opinion, and he virtually rejected its persuasiveness. He concluded that Judge Peckham's analysis never attacked what Judge Grady considered the threshold question—whether the tests were biased. Judge Grady believed that one could not arrive at a proper decision concerning the plaintiffs' claims in either case without examining the issue of test bias in detail. As for the California court's ultimate decision, Judge Grady merely said that "the witnesses and the arguments which persuaded Judge Peckham have not persuaded me" (p. 882).

The plaintiff school children appealed Judge Grady's decision. Ironically Chicago's new school board voluntarily decided to end individual intelligence testing for EMR placement as part of a schoolwide desegregation plan, thereby making the appeal unnecessary from the plaintiffs' perspective. The case is entangled in procedural maneuvers; an ultimate decision on appeal may never be reached.

Significance of Riles II and PASE

Undoubtedly in their disparate ways *Riles II* and *PASE* will have a significant effect on professional practice in the schools. Broadly interpreted, *Riles II* casts doubt on the continued utility of traditional psychometric evaluations using psychology's current storehouse of standardized ability tests. The court required the state to meet several validity criteria before it would approve continued administration of intelligence tests.

1. Tests would have to yield the same pattern of scores when administered to different groups of people.

2. Tests would have to yield approximately equal means of all subgroups included in the standardization sample.

3. Tests would have to be correlated with relevant concurrent or predictive measures.

The court rejected validity studies correlating IQ scores with college grades or with other achievement tests. As all the experts agreed that intelligence tests were merely achievement tests by another name, the court in *Riles II* held that studies comparing IQ scores with scores on labeled achievement tests spuriously inflated validity coefficients because of autocorrelation. The court would be satisfied only with research relating IQ scores of black children with classroom grades.

Given the court's definition of validity, probably no current intelligence test could meet the criteria for validity. It is unlikely that any psychological test, particularly the commonly used personality and projective instruments, would be acceptable to the court.

The most important disagreement between *Riles II* and *PASE* was their analyses of the allegation of cultural bias in the Wechsler Scales and the Stanford-Binet. Judge Peckham found the tests deficient on this ground; Judge Grady did not. The permanent injunction against the administration of individual intelligence tests to place black children in EMR classes in *Riles II* was based almost entirely on the court's conclusion that the tests were culturally biased. The persuasiveness of the court's opinion therefore depends almost entirely on the correctness of this finding. Regardless of whether one applauds or decries the result, there are unfortunate infirmities in the court's analysis. Similarly, Judge Grady's eventual holding that the black plaintiffs in *PASE* had failed to prove the tests discriminatory was based on his estimation of the absence of bias. The method by which he reached that judgment was embarrassingly devoid of intellectual integrity.

Although Judge Peckham rested his decision on the finding that the tests were culturally biased, he provided little hard data to support such a conclusion and was tentative in discussing it. In its 69-page printed opinion, the empirical support for the court's conclusions consumed only one page. Moreover, the court's determination that the tests contain questions biased against poor black children is not uniformly accepted; some data suggest that whatever discrimination exists in tests, lower scores in blacks result from content bias.

Efforts to produce culture-free tests or to reduce content bias have met with little success. "Nonverbal or performance tests are now generally recognized as falling short of the goal of freedom from cultural influences, and attempts to develop culture fair verbal tests . . . are recognized as failures" (Reschly, 1979, p. 231). More specifically, Anastasi (1976) states: "On the WISC, for instance, black children usually find the Performance Tests as difficult or more difficult than the Verbal tests; this pattern is also characteristic of children from low socioeconomic levels" (p. 348). Kirp (1973) concludes: "[I]t is sobering but instructive to recognize that minority children do poorly even on so-called culture-free tests" (p. 758).

There has been relatively little research on content bias itself, particularly with regard to individual intelligence tests. Results regarding standardized tests generally (Flaugher, 1978; Green, 1978) or individual intelligence tests specifically (Reschly, 1980; Reynolds, 1982; Sandoval, 1979) do not support Judge Peckham's conclusions.

If Judge Peckham's analysis of the issue of cultural bias is scanty and faulty, Judge Grady's can best be described as naive. At worst it is unintelligent and devoid of empirical content. At bottom what it represents is a single person's personal judgment cloaked in the apparent authority of judicial robes. The court's opinion in *PASE* amply supports Reschly's (1980) conclusion that, with regard to item bias in the individually administered intelligence tests, "subjective judgments appear to be unreliable and invalid in terms of empirical analysis. . . . The only data confirming test bias that exists now is judgmental and speculative" (p. 127).

What makes Judge Grady's opinion interesting, if not precedent setting, is that the published and easily accessible decision contains the questions and correct answers to every question on the WISC, WISC-R, and Stanford-Binet tests. Whether inadvertently or purposely, Judge Grady has given the test away. Although Judge Grady eventually upheld the tests as valid, his decision, to a far greater extent than Judge Peckham's in *Riles II*, may invalidate the tests. The security of these tests may have been seriously compromised, if not destroyed.

Minimum Competency Testing

Although the psycholegal aspects of the minimum competency testing movement have been the subject of some comment (e.g., Lerner, 1981; Lewis, 1979; Madaus & McDonagh, 1979; McClung, 1979), the movement has not received all the attention it deserves. Perhaps challenges to individual intelligence tests, which more directly affect the interests of professional psychologists and involve threats to one of psychology's most hallowed contributions, have preoccupied the attention of the field. However, the use of competency tests to determine eligibility for graduation, diploma, or both affects decidedly more test takers than the use of individual intelligence tests for placement in classes for the educably mentally retarded. The number of states using minimal competency tests changes rapidly; about 80 percent of the states have some kind of competency examination and about 50 percent use the test as a prerequisite for the award of a diploma (Lerner, 1981; Tuttle, 1980). Thus legal challenges to minimum competency tests may have more national significance than cases like *Larry P.* and *PASE*.

The first, and perhaps most important, case challenging minimum competency tests in the federal courts is *Debra P. v. Turlington* (1979, 1981), a class action on behalf of high-school seniors in Florida who had failed or would later fail the state's self-styled functional literacy test. Passing the test was a requisite for receiving a diploma; those who failed the test would receive only a certificate of completion if they met other requirements for graduation. The plaintiffs contended that the test was racially biased, was instituted without adequate notice that passing it would be necessary if the student wished a diploma, and would be used to resegregate the state's public schools through the use of remedial classes for those who failed the exam. Among the legal theories used to challenge use of the test were the familiar claims that it violated the

Equal Protection and Due Process clauses of the Constitution and Title VI of the 1964 Civil Rights Act.

When the lawsuit was filed, the test had been administered three times, with black students failing at disproportionately high rates. That finding, coupled with the fact that Florida's school systems were segregated by law until 1971, had a significant impact on the trial court's decision. The court acknowledged that the state had a legitimate interest in implementing a procedure to evaluate established educational objectives, but the court attributed the disparate impact on blacks to their inferior education in dual school systems. Thus, as in *Larry P.*, the court concluded that "race more than any other factor, including socioeconomic status, is a predictor of success on the test" (*Debra P. v. Turlington*, 1979, pp. 256–257) and that the test perpetuated past, purposeful discrimination. The court held that the use of the tests to deny diplomas violated the Equal Protection Clause and Title VI.

The court also agreed that the test violated due process. The students' expectation of a diploma was seen as a property interest protected by the Fourteenth Amendment. The labeling of those who failed the test as functional illiterates and their receipt of a certificate of completion instead of a diploma were seen as adverse stigmata infringing on the liberty component of due process. The court held that notice to students less than two years before implementation of the diploma sanction was inadequate to protect those constitutional interests. Such limited notice was insufficient to prepare for a statewide test for which there was no statewide curriculum.

However, the court disagreed that the use of remedial classes for those who failed the test violated the Constitution or federal statutes. Unlike the ability tracks in *Hobson* or the EMR classes in *Larry P.* and *PASE*, these classes were fluid, occupied only one third of the school day, and led to increasingly successful results for students preparing for reexamination. The court also cursorily brushed aside allegations that the test contained racially biased items.

Validity of the test. Most important for the present was the court's evaluation of the validity of the test. The test was a criterion-referenced assessment of mastery in 24 skill objectives in reading, writing, and arithmetic and in the solution of practical problems. Using as a basis for decision the *Standards for Educational and Psychological Tests* (APA et al., 1974)—hereafter referred to as *Test Standards*[1]—the court held that the test was both content and construct valid, that is, the test items adequately measured skill objectives and matched consensual definitions of functional illiteracy. Thus, although the timing of the test was condemned, the test was not.

Nevertheless, because of the lack of notice, the use of the test as a diploma-granting device was enjoined until the 1982–1983 school year, when all students in the state will have had access to a complete 12-year

[1] The *Test Standards* are under revision.

cycle of desegregated education. The state, however, was not precluded from using the test to assist in the identification and remediation of those who could not meet minimum skill objectives.

Both sides appealed the decision. Although the fifth circuit concurred with the judgment on almost all grounds (i.e., that the test was rationally related to a valid state interest and that it possessed construct validity), it disagreed on one major ground. It called the lower court's finding that the test was content valid "clearly erroneous" (*Debra P. v. Turlington*, 1981, p. 405). In the educational context, it defined content validity to mean curricular validity: "We believe that the state administered a test that was at least on the record before us, fundamentally unfair in that it *may* have covered matters not taught in the schools of the state" (p. 404, emphasis in original). The circuit court conceded that the test was probably a good match of what students should know but concluded that there was no evidence that the test measured what they had an opportunity to learn. The court of appeals remanded the case to the trial court to develop a record of proof that the "test administered measures what was actually taught in the schools of Florida" (p. 405). If the test failed to meet the curricular validity criterion, it would run afoul of the Constitution's requirement that state-imposed requirements infringing on protectible interests not be arbitrary or irrational. The parties are preparing for a trial on the issue of curricular match. The trial has been scheduled for early 1983, and no decision is expected until late spring of that year.[2]

One month after the fifth circuit decision in *Debra P.*, a federal district court in Georgia decided *Anderson v. Banks* (1981). In this case a county school district in 1978 instituted a requirement that all candidates for graduation must achieve a grade equivalency score of 9.0 in the mathematics and reading sections of the California Achievement Test in order to receive a diploma. Like the school system in Florida, the county had a history of purposeful discrimination; blacks and whites did not attend the same schools until 1970–1971. In that school year the county created a tracking system of placement, which appeared to be based on race rather than ability. A disproportionate number of black children were placed in the lower tracks, with a concomitant underrepresentation in higher ones, like *Hobson*, despite IQ scores comparable to students in other tracks.

As in *Debra P.* the test requirement for the granting of a diploma had an adverse and disproportionate impact on black students. There was one clear difference, however. In *Debra P.* the state used a locally developed minimum competency test; in *Anderson* the county used the California Achievement Test (CAT), which the plaintiffs conceded had been well received in the testing community and the construction and validation of which apparently met prevailing test standards. Although

[2]In May 1983, as this chapter was going to press, the trial court held that the use of the minimal competency test was constitutional and concluded that Florida could withhold high school diplomas from students who failed it.

the plaintiffs conceded that the CAT was generally useful, they claimed that the county performed no local validation studies; there were significant, often bizarre shifts in individual test scores over relatively short periods of retest time; and the examination did not measure what was being taught in the county schools.

The court discounted claims that the test had to be locally validated. It called the CAT "a test instrument constructed with the utmost care" (p. 508), not a precipitately constructed device. Its use, the court said, fostered legitimate state interests and resulted in significant benefit by inducing better academic performance and increased enthusiasm for learning.

> In *Debra P.*, the state hastily concocted an examination and implemented it in a statewide area in the space of slightly more than a year. [Here] . . . the school authorities selected a reliable and well-established test instrument. This appears to the court to be sound practice in that the school authorities took advantage of the expertise of professional test constructors rather than hastily put together their own instrument. (p. 509)

Ultimately the school system's use of the CAT ran into the same problem found dispositive in *Debra P.* The county's administration of tests for the purpose of issuing diplomas to children in racially segregated school systems with the correlative disparate impact on black children could be perceived as a means of perpetuating intentional discrimination. Even though there was no proof that the school imposed the diploma sanction purposely against blacks, the court concluded that "where the award of a diploma depends on the outcome of a test, the burden is on the school authorities to show that the test covered only material actually taught" (p. 509). This reasoning appears more related to curricular validity than to discrimination, an issue that the court did not directly address. The court used such reasoning to ban administration of the test only until June 1983, when all those graduating would be exposed to the unitary, desegregated system.

Other challenges. Challenges to minimal competency tests have not been limited to minority plaintiffs. Handicapped students, particularly the retarded, have also litigated the issue. The leading case is *Board of Education of Northport-East Northport Union Free School District v. Ambach* (1981), which was brought by two young adults, one suffering from a neurological impairment that affected her ability to do arithmetic computation, and the other a trainable mentally retarded man. Both had been awarded diplomas by the local school district, but neither had passed a basic skills test required by the New York Department of Education. The district was informed that, because of the requirement of the test, the district had violated state rules in granting the diplomas. Unlike prior cases the school district came to the defense of the students and complained that the denial of diplomas to handicapped children who could not pass the competency test would violate the Due Process and Equal Protection clauses of the Constitution, Section 504, and Public Law 94–142, as well as of the state constitution.

The state court held that New York had a legitimate interest in attempting to ensure the value of its diploma and that the use of minimal competency tests to effectuate those goals were within its power. The court also held that the diploma requirement did not violate Section 504 or Public Law 94–142: Although those acts require that handicapped students must be provided an appropriate education, they do not guarantee that such students will successfully achieve the academic level necessary for the award of a diploma. Finally, finding that the use of the test had a rational basis, the court refused to find that equal protection had been violated.

The only claim on which the handicapped students and the district prevailed was due process. Following *Debra P.* and *Anderson* the court held that the expectation of receipt of a diploma is a property interest and its denial has grave consequences. It held that the diploma sanction stigmatized those who failed and would be branded as second-rate students. Because of these protectable interests, the court concluded that the timeliness of notice to students violated fundamental fairness. Although the court did not explicitly agree with the testimony of one expert witness that handicapped students should be notified of the test requirement in the middle elementary school years, the court, without precisely stating what would be an appropriate date, asserted that "early notice would allow for proper consideration of whether the goals of the students [individual educational plan] should include preparation for the [basic competency test] and would afford an appropriate time for instruction aimed at reaching that goal" (pp. 574–575).

Although its holding implies that the court agrees with the curricular validity criterion, the court refused to rule on the claim that the minimal competency test did not accurately measure the basic skills of handicapped students. Although the students and the district claimed that the test did not meet the *Test Standards*, the court decided that judicial restraint prevented ruling on this issue—a constraint, however, that did not preclude a review of the validity of competency tests in other cases. Apparently the court found the due-process peg an easier and more comfortable place on which to hang its ruling than on the more complex issues of psychometric validity. In early 1983 an appellate court in New York affirmed the lesser court's decision.

Other courts have turned deaf ears to handicapped children's claims that the diploma sanction violates basic rights. The court in *Anderson*, for example, quoting the Supreme Court's decision in *Southeastern Community College v. Davis* (1979), said that "Section 504 imposes no requirement upon an educational institution to lower or to effect substantial modifications of standards to accommodate a handicapped person" (*Anderson v. Banks*, 1981, p. 511).

A decision highly antagonostic to claims by handicapped children that minimal competency tests are unfair is *Brookhart v. Illinois State Board of Education* (1982), the most recent case to consider the diploma sanction. Although the Illinois commissioner of education had ruled that the use of the test violated due process because a school system's adoption of the competency test requirement failed to give timely notice, a federal court disagreed. Although the requirement was instituted less than two years before taking effect, the court strongly upheld the district's right to use any reasonable means to determine the effectiveness of its education programs. Although the test had been locally developed, the court quickly brushed aside challenges to the validity of the test.

> Perhaps no test of human beings by human beings can always be scientifically exact, but that is not the measure. It is a reasonable test of the accomplishment of the school system in imparting basic knowledge to all its students, and unless some such measure is permitted, no certification of graduation from an educational program can have any meaning whatsoever, to the student or to others, as the notice of educational attainment is meant to be. (p. 728)

The court did acknowledge that failure to receive a diploma could be detrimental to handicapped students, but striking down the test requirement or forcing schools to modify the test to take into account mental and learning handicaps would foster only an inappropriate pretense of ability. Although it was aware that prior decisions took a more critical view of minimal competency tests, the court found such arguments unpersuasive. This case is on appeal. Counsel for the plaintiff asserts that, unlike those of the handicapped students in *Northport*, the child's handicap in this case was not severe and, with proper remediation, she could have passed the test. A decision is not expected for at least a year.

The case law in this area is still developing; to discern general principles is difficult. Often the decisions have failed to address significant issues. For example, students are distinguished as either literate or illiterate and may be denied the extremely significant credential of a diploma on the basis of one test. Both *Larry P.* and *PASE* agreed that special education placement and labeling must be based on a multifaceted assessment. Arguably the interests at stake in minimal competency testing are greater than those in the IQ testing cases. Yet the courts have never prohibited school systems from applying the diploma sanction on the basis of a single test score. The one identifiable trend—except for the decision in *Brookhart*—is toward using a curricular validity criterion to judge whether minimal competency tests pass legal muster. To withstand scrutiny, such tests may have to measure what students have been taught. This standard is much like the one in cases challenging employment tests, in which the courts have required some evidence of job relatedness.

Employment

Griggs and the Uniform Guidelines

The confusion and controversy surrounding educational tests may be matched in employment settings. Since the Supreme Court decided *Griggs v. Duke Power Co.* (1971), the first major challenge to employment tests, the issues have become sharper and more sophisticated. Although some relevant aspects of *Griggs* were described in the discussion of *Larry P.,* because *Griggs* is the landmark case, it may be helpful to review it in some detail.

Before 1965 the Duke Power Company openly discriminated on the basis of race in the hiring and assigning of employees at its Dan River plant. Blacks were employed only in the lowest level jobs and at the lowest rate of pay. In 1964 Congress passed the Civil Rights Act. In Title VII of the act Congress required the removal of artificial, arbitrary, and unnecessary barriers to employment. There are three pertinent sections to Title VII. In Section 703(a)(1) Congress made it "an unlawful employment practice for an employer . . . to fail or refuse to hire . . . any individual, or otherwise to discriminate against any individual with respect to his compensation, terms, conditions or privileges of employment, because of . . . race, color, religion, sex, or national origin." Section 703(a)(2) bans employment practices that would invidiously "limit, segregate, or classify . . . employees or applicants for employment in any way which would deprive or tend to deprive any individual of employment opportunities, or otherwise adversely effect his status as an employee." Despite these prohibitions Section 703(h) does permit the use of employment testing.

> Notwithstanding any other provision of this [title], it shall not be an unlawful employment practice for an employer . . . to give and to act upon the results of any professionally developed ability test provided that such test, its administration or action upon the results is not designed, intended or used to discriminate because of race, color, religion, sex or national origin.

The act applies to almost all medium and large private employers and, since its amendment in 1972, to municipal, state, and federal employers.

To enforce Title VII Congress combined both administrative and judicial methods. A person claiming to be the victim of discrimination must first file a charge with the Equal Employment Opportunity Commission (EEOC). The commission must then serve notice of the charge to the employer and begin an investigation to determine whether there is reasonable cause to believe the charge. If it finds no reasonable cause, EEOC must dismiss the charge. If it does find reasonable cause, EEOC must try to eliminate the alleged discriminatory practice through such informal means as conferences and conciliation.

If attempts at resolution fail, EEOC may bring a civil action against an employer. But Title VII also makes private lawsuits by aggrieved employees an important part of its enforcement mechanism. If EEOC dismisses the charge, the employee may immediately file a private action. Regardless of whether EEOC finds reasonable cause, the employee may bring an action 180 days after filing the charge if the commission has not filed its own lawsuit. Under EEOC regulations the employee may obtain a right-to-sue letter on request 180 days after filing the charge, but EEOC may issue a right-to-sue letter earlier if it finds that it cannot complete its investigation of the charge within the time limit. Employees then have 90 days from EEOC's notice of the right to sue to file a private action in court.

On July 2, 1965, the date on which Title VII took effect, Duke Power decided no longer to restrict blacks to the lowest level positions. However, it instituted a policy that, to qualify for placement in higher level positions, employees must achieve satisfactory scores on the Wonderlic Personnel Test, purportedly an intelligence measure, and the Bennett Mechanical Comprehension Test. Black employees challenged the tests under Title VII, claiming that neither instrument was intended to measure the ability to learn to perform a particular job or a category of jobs. The employer conceded that the tests may have had a prejudicial effect in that few blacks were employed or promoted but contended that the company had no intent to discriminate. A unanimous Supreme Court, however, interpreted Title VII as proscribing "not only overt discrimination but also practices that are fair in form, but discriminatory in operation" (p. 431). Once plaintiffs produced significant statistical evidence of a disproportionate impact on minorities, employers bore the burden of showing "that any given requirement . . . ha[d] a manifest relationship to the employment in question" (p. 432). The Court faulted the company for using "broad and general testing devices" (p. 433) and brushed aside the argument that the company was conforming to Title VII's approval of professionally developed ability tests to make employment decisions. The Court reminded the defendants that the EEOC *Guidelines on Employment Testing* (EEOC, 1966) defined such tests as ones that "fairly measure the knowledge or skills required by the particular job" and are supported by data indicating that the instruments used are "predictive of or significantly correlated with important elements of work behavior which comprise or are relevant to the job for which candidates are being evaluated" (29 C.F.R. §1607). Although the Court conceded that the guidelines did not have the force of law, they were "entitled to great deference" (p. 434). Thus, although tests are not precluded by the Civil Rights Act, they must "measure the person for the job and not the person in the abstract" (p. 436).

Griggs, then, introduced the concept of job-relatedness into the law of employment testing. But the Supreme Court did not develop distinct criteria by which employers could judge whether they had successfully achieved that goal. The Court had that opportunity in *Albemarle Paper Co. v. Moody* (1975). The Albemarle Paper Company hired an industrial psychologist to validate the company's use of general ability tests as a condition of employment. The psychologist compared test scores of current employees with supervisors' judgments of competence in several job groupings selected from the middle to top of the employer's skilled lines of progression. The Court found the study materially defective, condemning in particular the failure of the company to analyze "the attributes of, or the particular skills needed in, the study's job groups" (p. 432). In scrutinizing the tests, the Court again invoked the EEOC Guidelines but sought to bolster them by asserting that they drew on and made "reference to professional standards of test validation established by the American Psychological Association" (p. 431). The Court was referring to the *Test Standards.*

Issues Raised by Griggs

Griggs, and to a lesser extent, *Albemarle,* raised a number of issues, two of particular pertinence. The first issue concerns the extent to which the courts will use the EEOC Guidelines as controlling legal and psychological principles in deciding cases. Since their inception, the guidelines have been controversial. APA's Committee on Psychological Tests and Assessment has had a running battle with the commission concerning the guidelines' psychometric validity and practical utility. Psychologists in the Office of Personnel Management (OPM), an agency that administers millions of tests to prospective federal employees, have been at odds with their counterparts in EEOC. In fact, the government's own basic civil service test, the Professional and Administrative Career Examination (PACE), was voluntarily retired from service after minority plaintiffs claimed that the test was discriminatory.

Although a unanimous Supreme Court stated in *Griggs* (1971) that the EEOC Guidelines were "entitled to great deference" (p. 434), the decision in *Albermarle* was not unanimous. Chief Justice Berger and Justice Blackmun disagreed with the majority's reliance on the EEOC Guidelines. Justice Blackmun complained that the guidelines had not been subjected to adversary comment and should be given neither rigid application nor absolute compliance. The chief justice, though the author of *Griggs*, criticized the Court for its "slavish adherence" to the guidelines in fashioning criteria by which employers must prove job relatedness. The guidelines, he said, should be "entitled to the same weight as other well-founded testimony by experts in the field of employment testing" (p. 452).

In 1976 in *Washington v. Davis* the Court further reduced its reliance on the guidelines. Although the Court expanded its interpretation of the job-relatedness requirement in *Davis,* it referred to the guidelines in its decision only once in a footnote. Shortly thereafter, in *General Electric Co. v. Gilbert* (1976), a sex discrimination case (not involving the use of tests), the Court explicitly disregarded an EEOC guideline concerning pregnancy disability and indicated that administrative interpretations, like the guidelines, constituted merely "a body of experience and informed judgment to which courts and litigants may properly resort for guidance"; they did not control precedent (p. 141).

The guidelines were substantially revised after *Davis,* in 1976, and in 1978 a cooperative endeavor by EEOC, OPM, and the Departments of Justice, Treasury, and Labor produced the extant version, the *Uniform Guidelines on Employee Selection Procedures.* In 1979 and in 1980 these agencies published a set of "Questions and Answers," which they hoped would provide a common interpretation of the Uniform Guidelines (EEOC et al., 1979, 1980). The 1978 version of the guidelines has not been definitively discussed by the Supreme Court. The Supreme Court was invited to do so by defendants in *Connecticut v. Teal* (1982). In a long footnote the Court demurred, concluding that nothing in the guidelines would aid the defendant's argument and that interpretation of Title VII alone could resolve the issue.

The second issue raised by *Griggs* was the kind and quantity of proof necessary for minority plaintiffs to prevail in an employment testing case. *Griggs* established that plaintiffs could prevail if employer defendants could not show that employment tests were valid in the light of discriminatory impact or statistical disparity. However, the generalizability of that rule changed substantially when the Supreme Court decided *Washington v. Davis* (1976). In *Davis* the plaintiffs contended that a written personnel test used throughout the federal government and designed to measure verbal ability disproportionately excluded black applicants from positions in the District of Columbia Police Department. The case was litigated under the Equal Protection Clause of the Constitution rather than under Title VII, which had been used in *Griggs* and *Albemarle.* Seizing on that distinction, a majority of the Court held that claims of employment discrimination brought under the Constitution were not to be judged on the basis of discriminatory effect; plaintiffs would have to prove that the tests were intentionally used to foster discrimination.

The Court conceded that Title VII required that tests be

"validated" in terms of job performance in any one of several ways, perhaps by ascertaining the minimum skill, ability, or potential necessary for the position at issue and determining whether the qualifying tests are appropriate for the selection of qualified applicants for the job in question. (p. 247)

However, the Court found this rigorous standard inappropriate under the Constitution. It held that the employer would need to show merely a rational basis for the tests that it used. The Court agreed with the District's argument that basic knowledge of communication skills would be useful to predict satisfactory progress in police training and that the challenged tests were directly related to that requirement. Further, there was no need to validate the test by showing a positive relationship between the test and actual performance on the job; it would be sufficient to correlate the test with training performance.

Title VII Theory

Litigation under Title VII has now taken two tracks: disparate treatment and disparate impact (*McDonnell Douglas Corp. v. Green*, 1973; *Texas Dept. of Community Affairs v. Burdine*, 1981). Under both theories there are three common procedural requirements. First, the plaintiff must establish a prima facie case of employment discrimination, either by showing disparate treatment or effect. Second, if the plaintiff makes such a showing, the burden shifts to the defendant to prove or demonstrate a defense to the apparent discrimination. Third, if the defendant successfully rebuts the prima facie case, the burden then shifts to the plaintiff to show that there are available alternative, less discriminatory selection devices that would also serve the employer's legitimate interests in hiring or promoting effective workers.

There are differences between the two tracks, however. In a disparate treatment case the claim is that the employer treated the plaintiff less favorably than others because of race, color, religion, sex, or national origin. A plaintiff makes a prima facie case of disparate treatment by showing (1) that he or she belongs to one of the protected classes; (2) that he or she applied and was qualified for the job for which the employer was seeking applicants; (3) that despite his or her qualifications, he or she was rejected; and (4) that after the rejection, the position remained open, and the employer continued to seek applications from persons of the plaintiff's qualifications.

If the plaintiff succeeds in establishing a prima facie case by a preponderance of the evidence, then the burden shifts to the employer to articulate some legitimate, nondiscriminatory basis for the employee's rejection. Once the employer has rebutted the presumption created by the plaintiff's prima facie showing, the plaintiff is given the opportunity to show that the employer's stated reasons for rejection were merely a pretext for discrimination.

In disparate impact cases, however, there is no need to prove discriminatory motive. Under the disparate impact theory, an employee may challenge tests that appear neutral but fall more harshly on one of the protected groups. The plaintiff proves a prima facie case of discrimination by demonstrating that the employer's tests select applicants for hire or promotion in a racial, ethnic, or gender pattern significantly different from that of the pool of applicants. To rebut this showing, the employer must then prove that the test has some manifest relation to the job in question, that is, it is required by business necessity and is job related. Finally, if the employer meets that burden, the plaintiff has an opportunity to show that other tests or selection devices, without a similarly undesirable effect, would also serve the employer's legitimate business interests or that the employer was using the test as a pretext for discrimination. Thus, although Title VII permits employers to use tests,

> Congress in adding Section 703(h), intended only to make clear that tests that were *job related* would be permissible despite their disparate impact . . . . A nonjob-related test that has a disparate racial impact, and is used to "limit" or "classify" employees, is "used to discriminate" within the meaning of Title VII, whether or not it was "designed or intended" to have this effect and despite an employer's efforts to compensate for its discriminatory effect. (*Connecticut v. Teal,* 1982, p. 2533–34)

Recent cases. Two important employment discrimination cases were decided in 1982 by the Supreme Court's interpreting Title VII. In *General Telephone Co. v. Falcon* (1982) the Court held that, although EEOC may file class actions suits directly under Title VII, the act "contains no special authorization for class suits maintained by private parties" (p. 4640) unless individual plaintiffs seeking to represent a large class meet the strict federal rules for instituting those actions. Thus the Court refused to permit plaintiffs who could support a specific allegation of discrimination to represent a class of persons unless the plaintiff could show that the issues involved were common and typical of the class. Most pertinently, however, the Court indicated in a footnote that, if employers used biased testing procedures to evaluate groups of applicants or potential promotees, meeting the requirements of commonality and typicality would be much easier.

The second case, *Connecticut v. Teal* (1982), is of more general importance. The plaintiffs were four black provisional state employees who, when they sought to attain permanent status in their jobs as welfare eligibility supervisors, were obliged to participate in a selection process requiring a passing score on a written test. Those who passed the test became part of an eligibility pool from which the state would select successful applicants. The final determinations were made on the basis of a number of nontest criteria, for example, past work and recommendations.

The plaintiffs failed to achieve the cutoff score on the test that would have made them eligible for further consideration. The passing rate for blacks was 68 percent that of whites. The unsuccessful plaintiffs instituted a suit, claiming that the state's use of the test violated Title VII's Section 703(a)(2). One month before trial the state made its final selection: 23 percent of the eligible blacks and 13.5 percent of the eligible whites were promoted to supervisor. The actual promotion rate of blacks, therefore, was 169.5 percent the actual promotion rate of whites. Thus, although the end result of the state's selection process (the so-called bottom line) was nondiscriminatory to blacks as a class, the threshold testing component did not meet the Uniform Guidelines four-fifths rule, which provides that a "selection rate for any race, sex, or ethnic group which is less than [80 percent] of the rate for the group with the highest rate will generally be regarded . . . as evidence of adverse impact" (29 C.F.R. §1607.4 [c]).

The federal district court dismissed the plaintiffs' claims, holding that the plaintiffs failed to prove a prima facie case of disparate impact. The court asserted that, whereas the black *passing* rate was 68 percent the white passing rate, the black *appointment* rate was almost 170 percent the white appointment rate. Thus, under the bottom-line approach in the EEOC Guidelines, the plaintiffs' Title VII claim failed.

The plaintiffs appealed. The court of appeals reversed the lower court, holding that

> where a plaintiff establishes that a component of a selection process produced disparate results *and* constituted a pass-fail barrier beyond which the complaining candidates were not permitted to proceed, a prima facie case of disparate impact is established, not withstanding that the entire selection procedure did not yield disparate results. (*Teal v. Connecticut*, 1981, p. 135)

In concluding that the district court was wrong in ruling that the results of the written examination alone were insufficient to support a prima facie case of disparate impact, the court of appeals distinguished an earlier decision by the second circuit. In *Kirkland v. New York State Dept. of Correctional Services* (1975), the court of appeals held that proof concerning disparate impact of certain subtests within a larger examination did not constitute an unlawful discriminatory impact. But the second circuit said in *Kirkland* that all applicants were subjected to a complete selection process, which when viewed as a whole did not produce disparate results. In *Teal*, however, the pass-fail barrier denied employment opportunity to a disproportionately large number of minority candidates and prevented them from proceeding to the next step in the selection process. Thus, the court concluded, affirmative action policies that may benefit minority groups as a class do not excuse employers' discriminatory conduct affecting specific and readily identifiable individuals. It held that "Title VII was designed to protect the rights of individuals" and that it "matters very little to the victimized individuals that their group as a whole is well represented in the group of hirees" (pp. 139–140).

In June 1981 the state of Connecticut asked the Supreme Court to review the second circuit's opinion, arguing that its decision was antagonistic to that of other circuits, which had adopted the bottom-line concept in Title VII cases. The state asserted that scrutiny of testing practices for hiring or promotion with no disparate impact would redirect employers' concerns from "the overall hiring process to the testing process, and in that sense [the federal courts would] be restructuring business practices."

The Supreme Court agreed to review the case; in June 1982 it rendered its opinion. The Court held in a 5–4 decision that "the 'bottom line' did not preclude . . . employees from establishing a prima facie case [of employment discrimination] nor did it provide the employer with a defense to such a case" (*Connecticut v. Teal*, 1982, p. 2526). The Court reminded employers that Section 703(a)(2) spoke in terms not of jobs and promotions but of limitations and classifications that would deprive individuals of employment opportunities. Thus, "[w]hen an employer uses a nonjob-related barrier to deny a minority or woman applicant employment or promotion, and that barrier has a significant adverse effect on minorities or women, then the applicant has been deprived of an employment 'opportunity' because of . . . race, color, religion, sex, or national origin" (p. 2526). Therefore, Title VII protects individuals, not groups; it prohibits employers from telling victims of a policy with discriminatory effect that the victims have not been wronged simply because other persons of their race or sex were hired: "Every *individual* employee is protected against both discriminatory treatment and against practices that are fair in form but discriminatory in operation" (p. 2527; emphasis added).

As a result, the Court refused to permit employers to claim as a defense in disparate impact cases that discriminatory, non–job-related tests serving as a pass-fail barrier to employment opportunities are permissible because the tests did not actually deprive disproportionate numbers of blacks of promotions. "It is clear," the Court asserted, "that Congress never intended to give an employer license to discriminate against some employees on the basis of race or sex merely because he favorably treats other members of the employees' group" (p. 2535).

The dissenters, with Justice Powell speaking for the chief justice and Justices Rehnquist and O'Connor, agreed that the aim of Title VII was to protect individuals, not groups. However, they interpreted disparate impact claims as requiring proof of discrimination to groups. The dissenting opinion was that prior cases had made clear that discriminatory impact claims cannot be based on how an individual is treated because those claims are necessarily based on whether the group fares less well than other groups under a policy, practice, or test. The dissent warned that the majority's holding could "force employers either to eliminate tests or rely on expensive, job-related, testing procedures, the validity of which may or may not be sustained if challenged. For state and local governmental employers with limited funds, the practical effect of today's decision may well be the adoption of simple quota hiring" (pp. 2539–2540). Moreover, it cautioned, substantially fewer minority candidates could be hired by integrating test results into one overall hiring decision because then employers "will be free to select *only* the number of minority candidates proportional to their representation in the workforce" (p. 2540, n. 8).

The Court's approach to test validation. The Court's holding in *Teal* may have dissatisfied the dissenters; to the extent that the dissenters' prediction proves true, it may ultimately rebound to the detriment of large numbers of minorities and women. The majority's failure to rule on the legal status of the 1978 Uniform Guidelines and the implementing questions and answers may have also disappointed psychologists whose work in industrial and public service institutions is conducted with a wary eye on those documents. What has probably concerned measurement experts more generally has been the Court's muddled approach to test validation in all of its employment cases. The federal courts, EEOC, and psychometric experts have extreme differences of opinion as to the proper conceptualization of test validation within the industrial setting. Novick (1981) has perceptively summarized the struggle:

> Individual federal agencies have responsibilities and goals delegated by the executive and legislative branches of government, monitored by the judicial branch, and ultimately specified by the incumbent agency management. Although these agencies share concern for benefits to society as a whole, they tend to focus attention on their own particular mandates, and for this reason they often view testing and other issues quite differently. In fact, it is not uncommon for government agencies to be on opposite sides in litigation involving tests, for employers to receive conflicting directives from different government agencies, and for employees to find that their test scores are considered in light of widely varying objectives by employers and government agency representatives. (p. 1035)

In *Washington v. Davis*, supporting its opinion that validation could be accomplished in "any one of several ways," the Court cited the *APA*

Test Standards to the effect that there were "three basic methods of validation: 'empirical' or 'criterion' validity . . . , 'construct' validity . . . , and 'content' validity" (*Washington v. Davis,* 1976, p. 247, fn. 13). Many industrial and academic psychologists (Guion, 1980; Messick, 1980; Tenopyr, 1977) contend that insofar as the courts have interpreted the test standards and the EEOC Guidelines to mean that content, criterion, and construct validity are distinct forms of validation, those interpretations are oversimplified, if not erroneous. The Uniform Guidelines, according to this view, inappropriately treat three aspects of validity as "something of a holy trinity representing three different roads to psychometric salvation" (Guion, 1980, p. 386) rather than viewing them as subsets within the unifying and common framework of construct validity. It has been suggested that the term *construct-referenced validity* (Messick, 1975) would more precisely encompass almost all discrete and specialized validation terms, integrating content relevance and content coverage as well as predictive and diagnostic utility. "The bridge or unifying theme that permits this integration is the meaningfulness of interpretability of the test scores, which is the goal of the construct validation process" (Messick, 1980, p. 1015).

Federal view of validity. The federal government's view of validity is finding its way into judicial decisions concerning employment discrimination, most recently exemplified in *United States v. City of St. Louis* (1981). The original plaintiffs were the Justice Department and the Firefighters Institute for Racial Equality (FIRE), a class of black applicants for promotion to fire captain who challenged the use of selection devices that had produced racially disparate results. The case has volleyed between the federal district court and the Eighth Circuit Court of Appeals. Although the appellate court has upheld the city's use of content validation—even though criterion-related studies were feasible—it has continually condemned both the particular test used and the studies presented to support their validity.

The test at issue consisted of a written multiple-choice portion and simulation exercises (assessment center technique). The appellate court held that the multiple-choice test was not content valid because it primarily assessed reading and writing skills and, thus, was too dissimilar to the work situation in which fire captains would be placed. Because the city chose to use the results to rank candidates, the court held that devices on which rankings are based must be supported by empirical evidence that greater knowledge is positively linked to job performance. Although the multiple-choice test was developed by an expert panel, the court concluded that the items were based principally on "opinion and conjecture, not actual observation of the correlation between the extent of mastery of the knowledges and abilities sought to be measured by the test and job performance" (pp. 358–359).

The assessment center portion consisted of three parts: (1) a fire-scene simulation in which candidates are shown slides of a fire and asked to respond in writing to questions regarding their observations and potential commands; (2) a training simulation in which candidates present an informational lecture; and (3) an interview simulation in which candidates interact with a role-playing firefighter involved in a confrontation with a co-worker. Although the court found infirmities in each portion, it expressed most concern about the fire-scene simulation. The simulation was seen as a pencil-and-paper test, far removed from a fire captain's actual work and concerned with verbal skills, which are not critical for that position.

The city petitioned the Supreme Court for review and asked the justices to consider the appellate court's requirement of empirical evidence of validity. The city contended that the tests were professionally developed and proven to be job related. Because the city sought to rank candidates for promotion, the petitioners argued, the requirement of empirical evidence was inappropriate except for data showing a relation between the selection procedure and a complete job analysis. In mid-1981 the Supreme Court refused to hear the case, and the lower court's decision stands.

The possibility that the Court might hear the case worried many industrial psychologists who believed that the continued legality of content-oriented methods in employment selection would be threatened. The issue was raised in the context of an employer criticized by the courts for a history of purposely discriminating against minorities in the hiring and promotion of applicants for civil service jobs. There was concern that in holding the city's actions illegal the Court would have virtually condemned the use of content-oriented validity. The ultimate consequence of producing a conclusive presumption against this approach in the selection of applicants for skilled positions would have been the restriction of content validity solely to jobs in which pencil-and-paper tests were part of the job content domain; this situation would threaten the use of job-sampling tests and assessment in simulated situations.

On the same day the Supreme Court refused to review the appellate court's decision in *City of St. Louis,* it took the same action in *Guardians Association of New York City v. Civil Service Commission* (1981). *Guardians* is perhaps the most sophisticated opinion concerning validation of employment tests. Black applicants for positions as police officers contended that the city used content, rather than construct, validation for a test that was perceived to measure such attributes as intelligence, aptitude, personality, and leadership. The city countered that, unlike the defendants in *Griggs* or *Albemarle,* it had conscientiously performed extensive job analyses conforming to the Uniform Guidelines and that, despite the disparate impact against minorities produced by the test, the test validly measured the knowledge, skills, and abilities related to the job of police officer.

The appeals court saw the significance of the conflict between the plaintiffs and defendants. Because it is almost always more feasible to conduct content-oriented studies than the more data-oriented alternative of construct validity, "this content-construct distinction has a significance beyond just selecting the proper technique for validating the exam; it frequently determined who wins the lawsuit" (p. 92). The court took what it called a functional approach that would focus on the nature of the job. From the court's perspective the crucial question in analyzing cases brought under Title VII was "job-relatedness—whether or not the abilities being tested for are those that can be determined by direct, verifiable observation to be required or desirable for the job" (p. 93).

In applying the functional approach, the court said that it would be improper to rule out content-oriented methods simply because the position involved abilities that were somewhat abstract and could be characterized as constructs. The court criticized the Uniform Guidelines for adopting a rigid position inconsistent with Title VII's endorsement of professionally validated tests. Relying more on the published works of psychologists than on the guidelines, the court chose to cut through what it viewed as arbitrary distinctions among validation techniques. If the test measured general qualities relevant to many jobs, the court asserted that employers could be forced to use the more stringent procedure of construct validation. "But, as long as the abilities that the test attempts to measure are no more abstract then necessary, that is, as long as they are the most observable abilities of significance to the particular job in question, content validation should be available" (p. 93). Intelligence tests (like those challenged in *Griggs* and *Albemarle*), because they may be biased in favor of those from the dominant culture and because they measure highly abstract attributes, would almost always have to be validated empirically. The vast majority of the current generation of more job-related employment tests, however, could be judged on the content-construct continuum.

The court saw at least two beneficial consequences from its decision: (1) Content validation would not be relegated to only the most mundane tasks, such as typing; and (2) judges would not have to make a threshold decision between content and construct validation based solely on the nature of the quality tested without taking into account how that quality related to the job.

> Instead of choosing between content and construct validation at the outset, as the [Uniform] Guidelines seem to require, employers and the courts can start the content validation inquiry and use its results to determine whether content validation is appropriate and whether it has been achieved. (p. 93)

Although the court upheld the barring of the particular examination in question, it concluded that content-oriented methods were properly applied in assessing the police officer selection test.

Other Legal Theories

Although Title VII is the primary vehicle for challenges to testing practices in employment settings, it is by no means the sole vehicle. Employees may also bring claims under the Fourteenth Amendment when the state's action is challenged or under the Thirteenth Amendment, which bars discrimination by private entities. An outgrowth of those two constitutional restrictions is a federal civil rights statute, 42 U.S.C. Section 1981, which provides: "All persons within the jurisdiction of the United States shall have the same right in every State and Territory to make and enforce contracts, . . . and to the full and equal benefit of all laws and proceedings for the security of persons and property as is enjoyed by white citizens." Another applicable statute is 20 U.S.C. Section 1701, the Equal Educational Opportunity Act enacted in 1974, which bars "discrimination by an educational agency on the basis of race, color or national origin in employment . . . of faculty or staff." That statute has been used to challenge discriminatory hiring of minority teachers or promotions to administrative positions. Some employees have used the more general provision of the 1964 Civil Rights Act's Title VI to challenge selection devices. Title VI provides that "no person in the United States shall, on the ground of race, color, or national origin be excluded from participation in, be denied the benefits of, or be subjected to discrimination under any program or activity receiving federal financial assistance."

Because Title VII limits monetary relief to 2 years' back pay, cannot be used where there are fewer than 15 employees, and requires exhaustion of administrative remedies, some plaintiffs seeking unlimited back pay and punitive and compensatory damages have used alternative theories. However, claims under the Fourteenth Amendment require proof of discriminatory intent. Likewise, the Equal Educational Opportunity Act has been interpreted to require intent. In a recent decision the Supreme Court in *General Building Contractors Association v. Pennsylvania* (1982), held that Section 1981 also requires evidence of a discriminatory purpose. It has never decided whether the Thirteenth Amendment or Title VI does also. The Court raised the Thirteenth Amendment question in *General Contractors* but did not decide it. But it has decided to render an opinion regarding Title VI in 1983, when it hears another version of the *Guardians* case. Based on intimations from prior cases, especially *Regents of the University of California v. Bakke* (1978), the Court will probably rule that Title VI, unlike Title VII, requires proof of intent. All these alternate grounds, therefore, complicate proving discrimination. Proving bad purpose or motive is not as easy as showing statistical disparity.

Even this extended discussion of the use of tests in employment settings has not been able to touch on several other important issues such as differential validity, the statistical significance required by the courts in assessing criterion-related correlation coefficients, or the measurement of adverse impact. For these and other issues the reader is referred to such sources as Booth and MacKay (1980), Lerner (1977), Shoben (1978), and Wigdor (1982).

Disclosure of Test Materials

Since their inception, test questions and answers have been shrouded in secrecy to prevent public disclosure. In the past, APA members could have been expelled from the association or suffered lesser sanction if they violated the Code of Ethics provision (now changed) that limited access to psychological tests and other assessment devices to "persons with professional interest who will safeguard their use" (APA, 1963, p. 59). Congruent with other consumer-oriented disclosure laws (Robertson, 1980), however, test materials have recently become more accessible to examinees, although psychologists began to urge their greater availability in the early 1970s (McClelland, 1973; Trachtman, 1972).

Rights of Students

The first major federal legislation affecting public disclosure of tests was the Family Education Rights and Privacy Act (FERPA), enacted in 1974. The act and its implementing regulations published in 1976 provide in part that educational institutions receiving funds under programs administered by the Department of Education must allow parents (and eligible students) access to records directly related to their children and an opportunity to challenge those records in a hearing. Portions of FERPA were incorporated in Public Law 94–142 in order to provide parents of handicapped children the right to inspect and review all education records pertaining to the placement of their children in special education programs.

Whether test protocols are accessible under these laws is not altogether clear. Excluded from the definition of a record are papers "in the sole possession of the maker thereof, and . . . not accessible or revealed to any other individual" (34 C.F.R. §99.3). Although WISC-R or Stanford-Binet protocols are not usually shared by the psychologist, information from them is. Psychologists routinely attend case conferences of school personnel to discuss diagnoses and recommendations for placement at which they disclose results of testing and give examples of responses. Even if test givers maintain test records in their offices, protocols could be considered records because they have been revealed to others. Section 300.562 of the regulations implementing Public Law 94–142 requires that schools permit parents to inspect and review their children's records that are collected, maintained, and used by the school in its special education decision making. Psychologists' tests and test results are almost always used in this process and could be considered accessible.

This analysis has not found its way into a judicial opinion. In *Lora v. Board of Education* (1980) the court declared that "failure to provide parents with clinical records upon which recommendations for special . . . placements are made" (p. 1278) would violate due process because parents would be unable to prepare properly for hearings to contest placements. Unfortunately the court did not clarify what it meant by the term *clinical records*. However, the Office of Special Education and Rehabilitation Services of the Department of Education considers test protocols reviewable by parents under both FERPA and Public Law 94–142 (Office of Special Education, 1981; Irvin, Note 1), although schools are not required to make copies of tests unless parents are unable to visit the school to conduct a review or unless the records are to be submitted as evidence in hearings to challenge psychoeducational evaluations or placement.

The requirements of FERPA and Public Law 94–142 do not mean that psychologists' records are open for general inspection. *Gilliard v. Schmidt* (1978) exemplifies protection by the Constitution of privacy rights of psychologists and those with whom they work. In that case, a guidance counselor filed suit against a school-board member who had rifled through the counselor's desk one evening in attempt to discover whether the counselor had drawn a cartoon that ridiculed the school board and had been printed in a local newspaper. A federal court of appeals upheld the employee's right to sue the school-board member for violating his rights under the Fourth Amendment to be free from unreasonable government intrusion. The court reasoned that the counselor, working in an office that was secured by a locked door and that contained psychological tests and other confidential students records, had a reasonable expectation that papers in his desk would remain safe and private unless a published school-board policy specifically warned that employees' desks could be searched.

Rights of Employees

Employees have fared less well than schoolchildren in discovering the contents of tests and their results. In *Detroit Edison v. National Labor Relations Board* (1979) a union alleged that workers were wrongfully denied promotion after taking required aptitude tests. The union requested copies of the examinations as well as of the answers and scores of applicants, but the company supplied only sample questions, descriptive literature, and validation studies, arguing that greater disclosure would render the test unusable, compromise the confidentiality of its employees, and breach the ethical code of APA psychologists who had developed the tests. The administrative law judge who first heard the case permitted access contingent on the information being disclosed only to an industrial psychologist selected by the union. He also forbade the copying of the tests and their disclosure to third parties but ordered that test scores be given directly to the union. On review the National Labor Relations Board (NLRB) affirmed the decision in principle but amended it to allow both the tests and scores to go to the union. A federal appeals court affirmed that decision, dismissing contentions by APA in an amicus brief supporting the company that disclosure of the tests would ignore the interest of present and future examinees as well as psychologists.

However, the Supreme Court reversed the appellate tribunal, holding that NLRB's remedies for handling employee's grievance did not adequately protect test security.

> The finding by the Board that this concern did not outweigh the Union's interest in exploring the fairness of the Company's criteria for promotion did not carry with it any suggestion that the concern itself was not legitimate and substantial. Indeed, on this record— which has established the Company's freedom under the collective contract to use aptitude tests as a criterion for promotion, the empirical validity of the tests, and the relationship between secrecy and test validity—the strength of the Company's concern has been abundantly demonstrated. (p. 448)

The Court's ruling that direct disclosure of test scores to the union was inappropriate was based entirely on its desire to protect the rights of individual employees who had had no opportunity to consent to the disclosure. It noted APA's contention that breach of its ethical principles was an adequate ground for refusing to disclose test scores and also noted NLRB's competing position that a federal statutory duty to disclose relevant information could not be defeated by the code of ethics of a private association. But the Court ruled in favor of Detroit Edison because of the importance that it saw in the right of employees to prevent public scrutiny of sensitive information and because of the minimal burden placed on the union to obtain consent prior to such disclosure.

In the same year (1979) a federal appeals court denied a civil service applicant access to a multiple-choice examination. The government agency permitted inspection and review of the essay but not of the objective portion of the test. The court agreed the distinction was rational, concluding that essay tests were "much more susceptible to error and abuse than the automatic grading of multiple choice tests" (*Lavash v. Kountze*, 1979, p. 104). Perhaps more importantly, the court did not want to assume the role of "super personnel board" (p. 106), in which it would become embroiled in substantive challenges to the validity of examinations.

Truth in Testing

What applicants for employment and college admission may not be able to secure from the courts may ultimately be obtainable through legislation. New York and California in 1979 enacted so-called truth-in-testing laws; similar statutes have been proposed in several other states. California's law, the first, requires only that testing agencies supply sample questions to a state commission and general explanations of scoring mechanisms to test subjects. New York's law is far more stringent. In addition to provisions that set forth various requirements of notice and requirements of disclosure of test results by test agencies, the New York statutes impose certain obligations on test agencies with regard to disclosure of studies, background reports, and statistical data pertaining to the tests and, most pertinently, of the contents of the tests.

The most problematic provision is the last. Section 342 requires the test agency to file a copy of all test questions used in calculating a test taker's raw score and the corresponding correct answers within 30 days after the results of the test are released (experimental and equating items are exempt if they do not affect the test taker's raw score). Thereafter, on request of a test taker, the agency is required to send to the requester a copy of the test questions, the person's individual answer sheet, and a copy of the correct answer sheet. The statute was passed despite protests from the Educational Testing Service (ETS) and others claiming that it would violate test security, increase administrative costs, and work to the advantage of minorities and the handicapped. ETS and the other groups have since reduced their resistance to such laws.

Before the New York law went into effect, a preliminary injunction barring its implementation was sought by the Association of American Medical Colleges (*AAMC v. Carey*, 1981), the developer of the Medical College Admissions Test (MCAT). In seeking to enjoin enforcement of the law, AAMC alleged that disclosure requirements violated the federal copyright act and the Constitution. With regard to the former, the association claimed that its rights under the copyright act would be preempted by the state truth-in-testing law requiring disclosure under threat of civil penalty. With regard to the constitutional claim, the association argued that in effect New York was virtually destroying a valuable property interest in its tests and studies without just compensation and in violation of due process. The court found that the plaintiffs had presented sufficiently serious questions and could suffer irreparable injury should the test items be disclosed; therefore, the court barred enforcement of the law with regard to the MCAT until a full trial on that test's merits. At that time there would be an opportunity to weigh the state's competing claims that the law was enacted in the public interest to make testing agencies more accountable to the public and to reduce cultural biases from the tests, concerns that justified otherwise protected material on the basis of fair use.

No trial has been held; apparently the state has decided to continue MCAT's exemption from the law's requirements. However, some legal commentators agree that truth-in-testing laws serve public interests significantly enough to outweigh the commercial interests of test publishers. These commentators assert that test agencies retain almost total control over the production of assessment devices on which entrance to restricted educational, employment, and professional opportunities is based; this kind of natural monopoly justifies close government scrutiny and regulation. In that light, laws like New York's

> recognize the generalized public interest in assuring that tests are valid, unbiased, and effective predictors of later academic success. By requiring disclosure of testing materials, the state enables all interest groups to scrutinize the use of potential abuse more closely than was previously possible. Although the law does not directly regulate the content of the examinations, it attempts, by exposing them to criticism and independent reveiw, to encourage the agencies to develop better tests. The knowledge of test questions gained through disclosure is thus an indispensable mechanism to encourage test agencies to respond to public concerns. (Samuels, 1981, p. 190)

Congress has since 1979 considered passage of truth-in-testing laws. At least two bills were introduced in the House of Representatives in 1982. One, limited to admissions tests, would provide students with access to their correct answer sheets. Another would not require disclosure of test content but would be applicable to both educational and employment tests and professional licensing examinations. Neither bill was acted upon.

Despite the flurry of activity and the controversy that the enacted and proposed statutes have generated, neither their proponents' nor their opponents' predictions appear to have come true. A surprisingly small percentage of test takers have requested disclosure of materials; for example, in 1981–1982 only 3 percent of those taking the Graduate Record Examination (GRE) requested their scores (APA Committee on Psychological Tests and Assessment, Note 2). Although costs are greater and have been passed on to the consumer, the increase has been relatedly minimal and could be explained by inflation (APA, Note 2). Whatever the particular merits of these laws, they do represent a movement toward greater involvement of clients, subjects, examinees, and consumers of psychological services in their own evaluation and treatment (Fischer & Brodsky, 1978).

Conclusion

Legal scrutiny of psychological testing is both a present and a future reality. Although the legal system has often been misguided and naive in its judgments about testing, at least three benefits have resulted from the increased involvement of courts and legislatures in psychologists' testing practices. First, the involvement has made psychologists, as well as society, more sensitive to racial and cultural differences and to the ways in which apparently innocent and benign practices may perpetuate discrimination. Second, it has alerted psychologists to the fact that they will be held responsible for their conduct. To protect the rights of test takers, to safeguard their own integrity, and in the long run to serve the legitimate goals of their employers, psychologists must examine their practices, their interpretations, and their ultimate recommendations. Finally, the attack on psychological testing has accelerated the search for both improved and alternative means of assessment so that what is said about examinees more validly and truly depicts their perceptions of themselves and how they function in all spheres of life. The intense examination that psychological assessment has received from the legal system should be viewed as both salutary and welcome.

Reference Notes

1. Irvin, T. Letter to William Hafner, January 9, 1979.
2. American Psychological Association, Committee on Psychological Tests and Assessment. Statement on "Truth in Testing" Legislation, 1982.

References

Albemarle Paper Co. v. Moody, 422 U.S. 405 (1975).
American Psychological Association. Ethical standards of psychologists. *American Psychologist,* 1963, *18,* 56–60.
American Psychological Association, American Educational Research Association, & National Council on Measurement in Education. *Standards for educational and psychological tests.* Washington, D.C.: American Psychological Association, 1966.
American Psychological Association, American Educational Research Association, & National Council on Measurement in Education. *Standards for educational and psychological tests.* Washington, D.C.: American Psychological Association, 1974.
Amrine, M. (Ed.). Testing and public policy. *American Psychologist,* 1965, *20,* 857–992.
Anastasi, A. *Psychological testing* (4th ed.). New York: Macmillan, 1976.
Anderson v. Banks, 520 F. Supp. 472 (N.D. Ga. 1981).
Association of Am. Medical Colleges v. Carey, 482 F. Supp. 1358 (N.D. N.Y. 1981).

Bd. of Educ. of Northport-East Northport Union Free School Dist. v. Ambach, 436 NYS.2d 564 (Sup. Ct. 1981).

Berk, R., Bridges, W., & Shih, A. Does IQ really matter? A study of the use of IQ scores for the tracking of the mentally retarded. *American Sociological Review*, 1981, *46*, 58–71.

Bersoff, D. Silk purses into sow's ears: The decline of psychological testing and a suggestion for its redemption. *American Psychologist*, 1973, *28*, 842–849.

Bersoff, D. Regarding psychologists testily: Legal regulation of psychological assessment in the public schools. *Maryland Law Review*, 1979, *39*, 27–120.

Bersoff, D. Testing and the law. *American Psychologist*, 1981, *36*, 1047–1056.

Bersoff, D. The legal regulation of school psychology. In C. Reynolds & T. Gutkin (Eds.), *The handbook of school psychology.* New York: Wiley, 1982 (a).

Bersoff, D. Larry P. and PASE: Judicial report cards on the validity of individual intelligence tests. In T. Kratochwill (Ed.), *Advances in school psychology* (Vol. 2). Hillsdale, N.J.: Erlbaum, 1982 (b).

Bersoff, D. Social and legal influences on test development and usage. In B. Plake & S. Hansen (Eds.), *Buros-Nebraska Symposium on Measurement and Testing.* Lincoln, Neb.: University of Nebraska Press, in press.

Black, H. *They shall not pass.* New York: Morrow, 1963.

Booth, D., & MacKay, J. Legal constraints on employment testing and evolving trends in the law. *Emory Law Journal*, 1980, *29*, 121–194.

Brookhart v. Illinois State Bd. of Educ., 534 F. Supp. 725 (C.D. Ill. 1982).

Brown v. Bd. of Educ., 347 U.S. 483 (1954).

Cleary, A., Humphreys, L., Kendrick, S., & Wesman, A. Educational uses of tests with disadvantaged students. *American Psychologist*, 1975, *30*, 15–41.

Connecticut v. Teal, _____ U.S. _____, 102 S.Ct. 2525 (1982).

Covarrubias v. San Diego Unified School Dist., Civ. No. 70-394-S (S.D. Cal., filed Feb. 10, 1971).

Cronbach, L. Five decades of public controversy over mental testing. *American Psychologist*, 1975, *30*, 1–14.

Debra P. v. Turlington, 474 F. Supp. 244 (M.D. Fla. 1979), *aff'd in part and vacated in part and remanded,* 644 F.2d 397 (5th Cir. 1981).

Detroit Edison v. NLRB, 440 U.S. 301 (1979).

Diana v. State Bd. of Educ., C.A. No. C-70-73 R.F.P. (N.D. Cal. filed Aug. 9, 1971).

Equal Employment Opportunity Commission. *Guidelines on Employee Selection Procedures.* Washington, D.C.: Equal Employment Opportunity Commission, August 24, 1966. (29 C.F.R. § 1607).

Equal Employment Opportunity Commission, Civil Service Commission, Department of Labor, & Department of Justice. Adoption by four agencies of Uniform Guidelines on Employee Selection Procedures. *Federal Register*, 1978, *43*, 38290–38315.

Equal Employment Opportunity Commission, Office of Personnel Management, Department of Justice, Department of Labor, & Department of Treasury. Adoption of questions and answers to clarify and provide a common interpretation of the Uniform Guidelines on Employee Selection Procedures. *Federal Register*, 1979, *44*, 11996–12009.

Equal Employment Opportunity Commission, Office of Personnel Management, Department of Justice, Department of the Treasury, & Department of Labor. Adoption of additional questions and answers to clarify and provide a common interpretation of the Uniform Guidelines on Employee Selection Procedures. *Federal Register*, 1980, *45*, 29529–29531.

Fischer, C., & Brodsky, S. *The Prometheus principle: Informed participation by clients in human services.* New Brunswick, N.J.: Transaction, 1978.

Flaugher, R. The many definitions of test bias. *American Psychologist,* 1978, *33,* 671–679.

General Bldg. Contractors Ass'n v. Pennsylvania _____ U.S. _____, 102 S.Ct. 3141 (1982).

General Electric Co. v. Gilbert 429 U.S. 125 (1976).

General Telephone Co. v. Falcon, _____ U.S. _____, 102 S.Ct. 2364 (1982).

Gillard v. Schmidt, 579 F.2d 825 (2d Cir. 1978).

Glaser, R., & Bond, L. (Eds.). Testing: Concepts, policy, practice, and research. *American Psychologist,* 1981, *36,* 997–1206.

Goldman, R., & Hartig, L. The WISC may not be a valid predictor of school performance for primary-grade minority children. *American Journal of Mental Deficiency,* 1976, *80,* 583–587.

Green, B. In defense of measurement. *American Psychologist,* 1978, *33,* 664–670.

Griggs v. Duke Power Co., 401 U.S. 424 (1971).

Gross, M. *The brain watchers.* New York: Random House, 1962.

Guadalupe Organization, Inc. v. Tempe School District No. 3, Civ. No. 71-435 (D. Ariz. filed Aug. 9, 1971).

Guardians Ass'n of New York City v. Civil Serv. Comm'n, 630 F.2d 79 (2d Cir. 1980), *cert. denied,* 452 U.S. 939 (1981).

Guion, R. On trinitarian doctrines of validity. *Professional Psychology,* 1980, *11,* 385–398.

Haney, W. Validity, vaudeville, and values. *American Psychologist,* 1981, *36,* 1021–1024.

Heller, K., Holtzman, W., & Messick, S. *Placing children in special education: A strategy for equity.* Washington, D.C.: National Academy Press, 1982.

Hobson v. Hansen, 269 F. Supp. 401 (D. D.C. 1967) *aff'd sub. nom.* Smuck v. Hobson, 408 F.2d 175 (D.C. Cir. 1969).

Hoffman, B. *The tyranny of testing.* New York: Crowell-Collier, 1962.

Jensen, A. How much can we boost IQ and scholastic achievement? *Harvard Educational Review.* 1969, *39,* 1–123.

Jensen, A. *Bias in mental testing.* New York: Free Press, 1980.

Kamin, L. *The science and politics of IQ.* New York: Wiley, 1974.

Kirkland v. New York State Dep't of Correctional Services, 520 F.2d 420 (2d Cir. 1975) *cert. denied,* 429 U.S. 823 (1976).

Kirp, D. Schools as sorters: The constitutional and policy implications of student classification. *University of Pennsylvania Law Review,* 1973, *121,* 705–797.

Larry P. v. Riles, 343 F. Supp. 1306 (N.D. Cal. 1972) (order granting preliminary injunction) *aff'd* 502 F.2d 963 (9th Cir. 1974); 495 F. Supp. 926 (N.D. Cal. 1979) *appeal docketed,* No. 80-4027 (9th Cir., Jan. 17, 1980).

Lavash v. Kountze, 604 F.2d 103 (1st Cir. 1979).

Lerner, B. Washington v. Davis: Quantity, quality, and equality in employment testing. In P. Kurland (Ed.), *Supreme Court Review.* Chicago: University of Chicago Press, 1977.

Lerner, B. The minimum competence testing movement: Social, scientific and legal implications. *American Psychologist,* 1981, *36,* 1057–1066.

Lewis, P. Certifying functional literacy: Competency testing and implications for due process and equal educational opportunity. *Journal of Law and Education,* 1979, *8,* 145–163.

Lippman, W. The abuse of tests. *New Republic.* 1922, *32,* 297–298.

Lora v. Bd. of Educ., 456 F. Supp. 1211 (E.D.N.Y. 1979) *vacated and remanded on other grounds,* 623 F.2d 248 (2d Cir. 1980).

Madaus, G., & McDonagh, J. Minimum competency testing: Unexamined assumptions and unexplored negative outcomes. *New Directions for Testing and Measurement: Impactive Changes on Measurement,* 1979, *3,* 1–14.

McClelland, D. Testing for competence rather than for intelligence. *American Psychologist,* 1973, *28,* 1–14.

McClung, M. Competency testing programs: Legal and educational issues. *Fordham Law Review,* 1979, *47,* 651–702.

McDonnell Douglas Corp. v. Green, 411 U.S. 792 (1973).

Merriken v. Cressman 364 F. Supp. 913 (E.D. Pa. 1973).

Messé, L., Crano, W., Messé, S., & Rice, W. Evaluation of the predictive validity of tests of mental ability for classrooms performance in elementary grades. *Journal of Educational Psychology,* 1979, *71,* 233–241.

Messick, S. The standard problem: Meaning and values in measurement and evaluation. *American Psychologist,* 1975, *30,* 955–966.

Messick, S. Test validity and the ethics of assessment. *American Psychologist,* 1980, *35,* 1012–1027.

Meyers, C., MacMillan, D., & Yoshida, R. Validity of psychologists' identification of EMR students in the perspective of the California decertification experience. *Journal of School Psychology,* 1978, *16,* 3–15.

Neuberger, E. Intelligence tests: To be or not to be under the Education for All Handicapped Children Act of 1975. *Northwestern University Law Review,* 1981, *76,* 640–668.

Novick, M. Federal guidelines and professional standards. *American Psychologist,* 1981, *36,* 1035–1046.

Office of Special Education, Department of Education. Letter to John Kelley. Reprinted in *Education of the Handicapped Law Report,* 1981, *21,* 211:240–242.

PASE v. Hannon, 506 F. Supp. 831 (N.D. Ill. 1980).

Regents of the Univ. of Calif. v. Bakke 438 U.S. 265 (1978).

Reschly, D. Nonbiased assessment. In G. Phye & D. Reschly (Eds.), *School psychology: Perspectives and issues.* New York: Academic Press, 1979.

Reschly, D. Psychological evidence in the Larry P. opinion: A case of right problem— wrong solution? *School Psychology Review,* 1980, *9,* 123–135.

Reynolds, C. The problem of bias in psychological assessment. In C. Reynolds & T. Gutkin (Eds.), *The handbook of school psychology.* New York: Wiley, 1982.

Robertson, D. Examining the examiners: The trend toward truth in testing. *Journal of Law & Education,* 1980, *9,* 167–199.

Samuels, J. Testing truth-in-testing laws: Copyright and constitutional claims. *Columbia Law Review,* 1981, *81,* 179–198.

San Antonio Ind. Sch. Dist. v. Rodriguez, 411 U.S. 1 (1973).

Sandoval, J. The WISC-R and internal evidence of test bias and minority groups. *Journal of Counseling and Clinical Psychology,* 1979, *47,* 919–927.

Sherman, S., & Robinson, N. (Eds.). *Ability testing of handicapped people: Dilemma for government, science and the public.* Washington, D.C.: National Academy Press, 1982.

Shoben, E. Differential pass-fail rates in employment testing: Statistical proof under Title VII. *Harvard Law Review,* 1978, *91,* 793–813.

Smith, E. Test validation in the schools. *Texas Law Review,* 1980, *58,* 1123–1159.

Southeastern Comm. College v. Davis, 442 U.S. 397 (1979).

Stell v. Savannah-Chatham City Board of Education, 220 F. Supp., 667 (S.D. Ga. 1963) *rev'd,* 333 F.2d 55 (5th Cir.), *cert. denied,* 379 U.S. 933 (1964).

Tenopyr, M. Content-construct confusion. *Personnel Psychology,* 1977, *30,* 47–54.

Texas Dept. of Community Affairs v. Burdine, 450 U.S. 248 (1981).

Trachtman, G. Pupils, parents, privacy, and the school psychologist. *American Psychologist,* 1972, *27,* 32–45.

Tuttle, S. Education and the law: Functional literacy program—a matter of timing. *Stetson Law Review,* 1980, *10,* 125–139.

United States v. City of St. Louis, 616 F.2d 350 (8th Cir. 1980), *cert. denied* 452 U.S. 938 (1981).

Washington v. Davis, 426 U.S. 229 (1976).

Wigdor, A. Psychological testing and the law of employment discrimination. In A. Wigdor & W. Garner (Eds.), *Ability testing: Uses, consequences, and controversies.* Washington, D.C.: National Academy Press, 1982.

Wigdor, A., & Garner, W. (Eds.). *Ability testing: Uses, consequences, and controversies.* Washington, D.C.: National Academy Press, 1982.

Williams, R. Black pride, academic relevance & individual achievement. *Counseling Psychology,* 1970, *2,* 18–22.

DAVID L. ROSENHAN

PSYCHOLOGICAL ABNORMALITY AND LAW

D avid L. Rosenhan, professor of psychology and law at Stanford University, received his doctorate from Columbia University. He served as director of research at Elmhurst General Hospital, Elmhurst, New York, and research psychologist at the Center for Psychological Studies, Educational Testing Service. He has been lecturer, assistant professor, professor, and visiting professor at several American universities and was a visiting fellow at the Center for Socio-Legal Studies at Oxford University.

Rosenhan is a fellow of the American Psychological Association and of the American Association for the Advancement of Science. He is a member of the American Psychology-Law Society and past president of the American Board of Forensic Psychology, the Law and Society Association. He serves as president of APA's Division 41 (Psychology and Law).

Rosenhan has served as a consulting editor for several professional journals and publications, as an advisory editor for Holt, Rinehart & Winston, and as a member of the Clinical Projects Research Review Committee, National Institute of Mental Health. He has published four books and numerous articles in his areas of interest, which are abnormal psychology, the social and cognitive effects of emotional states, the development of altruism and character, and psychology and law.

DAVID L. ROSENHAN

PSYCHOLOGICAL ABNORMALITY AND LAW

The marriage between psychology and the law, which the 1982 Master Lecture Series celebrates, must be a union graced by the gods, for ordinary mortals would have neither predicted nor blessed it. I should never have thought to introduce those two, much less make the match. When I think of law, I think of dusty tomes. When I think of psychology, I think of people. Even experimental psychologists, who used to think of animals when they thought of psychology, now think of people. No psychologist—social, clinical, or experimental—associates libraries and dusty books when thinking of psychology. Evidence for that assertion can be found in any psychological paper citing references only to 1979. References earlier than 1975 are considered a pretentious display of scholarship and precedence.

Precedence, too, makes this union between psychology and law such an unlikely one. In law nearly everything is precedence. If someone has not said it, it is not only not worth saying, it is quite obviously wrong. There will never be a Nobel prize in law, because Nobel prizes are awarded for originality and the law abhors original ideas. Psychology, however, loves them. Being original is so important to psychologists that they rarely build on the work of another. Freud had barely

This research was supported by the Stanford Legal Research Fund, made possible by a bequest from the estate of Ira S. Lillick and by gifts from Roderick E. and Carla A. Hills and other friends of the Stanford Law School.

finished his monumental work on the mind when Adler, Jung, and Sullivan were hard at work developing their own approaches. In psychology, repeating someone else's observations (not to speak of replicating someone else's experiment) is considered the lowest form of scholarship, barely acceptable from an undergraduate and, surely, the kiss of death for a second-year graduate student.

Finally, in their methods of understanding the universe that they occupy, psychology and law are worlds apart. Lawyers could well spend their time speculating wisely on the number of teeth in a horse's mouth without ever going out to count them, to borrow from Francis Bacon. Psychologists, on the contrary, would be the first to say that this is no way to make progress. Not only must one count the teeth, but merely counting the teeth in one horse's mouth will gain little. What is needed is a stratified sample of horses' mouths that generates a reasonably precise distribution of horse's teeth in the universe of extant horses. A psychologist might suggest also measuring, for little extra cost, the size of the teeth, their location in the mouth, and their relation to a whole host of personality traits: proneness to violence, androgyny, and tendency to win, place, or show among them.

It is hard to know how they came together, these two odd characters, and harder still to understand how they weathered those first few years of marriage, so little did they have in common. Oracles predicted that they would not survive. Wigmore (1909), that eminent student of the law of evidence, had a pinched and critical view of the little that he had seen of the union in the work of Harvard's Münsterberg and doubted that the union would survive the ultimate test: producing intellectual progeny. He was wrong. The union has had its difficulties, as one might expect from the marriage of two such oddly matched disciplines. But perhaps because of its psychological and genetic diversity, it has produced remarkable offspring. To end this metaphor, these offspring have established a vigorous and diverse domain.

The domain of psychology and the law is quite possibly the broadest interface between the social sciences and the humanities. There are relatively few aspects of law to which psychology is not relevant and to which psychology does not contribute an especially interesting perspective. Whether it is constitutional law, torts, contracts, trusts and estates, corporate or antitrust law, discrimination or labor law—not to mention the more traditional areas of criminal, mental health, and family law—psychological theory, research, and practice are relevant and often illuminating. The size of the domain complicates sampling all of the issues that reside within the psychology-law hegemony. Even the topic of this paper—psychological abnormality and law—raises far more issues than can be covered here.

But comprehensiveness is not mandated here so much as intellectual excitement. For if psychology contributes wonderfully of its store of knowledge to the legal arena, if psychology often sharply casts legal questions in challenging formats, then law amply repays psychology in two ways. First, law has a striking way of infusing psychological issues with vigor, meaning, and immediacy. Second, law has an uncanny sense of psychology's Achilles' heels. Law often ferrets out precisely those theoretical and empirical issues that psychology has failed to resolve. For many of us, those are questions not carefully examined since graduate school and abandoned for other, more interesting tasks. Law has an insidious way of reminding us that those issues remain important and that we must press for their resolution.

Abnormality and Law

Many of the theoretical issues in psychology that are generally significant for law are particularly significant for the area of psychological abnormality and the law. For example, let us consider the defendant's state of mind at the time a crime was allegedly committed. Even with a skillful examiner, can the state of mind ever be properly assessed by later examining the defendant? That question is important for clinical forensic psychologists. The answer depends on whether one believes that memory is a tabula rasa or, alternately, that memory is reconstructive rather than substantive, such that one's memories of the past depend heavily one one's *present* cognitions, motives, intentions, and desires (Anderson & Bower, 1973; Bower, 1981). The latter view makes the prognosis for that investigative enterprise pessimistic.

We might consider the psychological issues concerning such thorny legal problems as the right to treatment and the right to refuse treatment. What, in the first place, is a treatment? Who defines it? Is rest and recreation a treatment? Does mere hospitalization, without more, qualify? Can the notion of positive treatment be asserted without recourse to side effects and aversiveness, and, if so, does brutalization qualify as treatment so long as it results in positive change, even some of the time?

These are two examples of the way in which law presses psychology to refine its views and develop theoretical clarity. We encounter these examples as we examine four significant issues in the domain of psychological abnormality and law:
- the insanity defense,
- child custody,
- the psychotherapist's duty to protect patients, and
- the potential abuse of clinical psychology and psychiatry by the state and by society.

These issues reflect the diversity of the domain of psychology and the law. They are not theoretically related, yet they are the kinds of problems that clinical forensic psychologists are called on to deal with every day. These topics point up some of the more interesting psychological and legal aspects. The importance of these topics varies with a host of social and legal circumstances.

The Insanity Defense

Whether the insanity defense deserves the seat of honor that it is often accorded in discussions of clinical issues and the law, at least for a while, it has had that position of prominence as a result of the 1982 trial of John W. Hinckley, Jr. I will not add to the store of knowledge on the trial, verdict, or commentary, nor take a position in the eddy of debate that surrounds the insanity defense itself. I can hardly imagine a civilized society that would *not* consider mental state when assessing guilt; as a result, I am relatively impervious to arguments against some form of insanity defense. But several observations might be made in this discussion, some relatively original, others merely useful.

Let us begin with a case from a recent essay by Charles Meyers.

A pretty young woman in her early thirties, a psychiatric outpatient with a history of several past hospitalizations, is prescribed antipsychotic medications, but complains that the medicine makes her feel sluggish, stiff and not herself. She decides that medicine is unnatural, and that henceforth she will eat only food that God provides, not chemicals. She throws away her pills and feels better almost immediately. She begins to understand things she could only sense vaguely before. The modern world has lost its connection with the natural order of things. Human beings were created in God's image, the Earth was given to them by Him as their garden. All the plants and animals were put in the garden to be enjoyed and exploited by God's children. Among the animals were creatures that mimicked the form of men, including apes, Negroes and orientals. The only true human beings were the white race, who were created on another planet and came to earth as space voyagers and colonists. Somehow this history has been lost and humans have lost sight of their origins. Indigenous fauna are vying for supremacy with the extraterrestrial cosmonauts.

Nature now begins to talk to the young woman directly and tells her what must be done to redress the balance. Someone must remind the colonists of their true destiny. She has been chosen. If she kills a Black the scales will fall from the eyes of the colonists and they will reperceive the natural order of things. She tries to resist doing it. She is weak. She is afraid she will be beaten and tortured by those who do not understand. But she cannot shirk her moral obligations. She entices a five year old black child to a deserted spot, strangles him and buries the body. Her precautions to avoid detection are clumsy and ineffectual, and she is arrested at her mother's home the next day. With nervous pride, she tells one of the arresting officers, "I killed a nigger." (Meyers, 1982 pp. 3–4)

Meyers' case is not uncommon in the annals of forensic psychology. Nevertheless, it continues to evoke both interest and sympathy in readers and listeners. I would suspect that even among those who have reservations about the insanity defense, this attractive young woman with a history of several previous psychiatric hospitalizations would have been a prime candidate for such a defense. Moreover, if her defense had failed, there would be a strong sense that justice had somehow miscarried.

Guilt and Seriousness

Why should there be such a sense of certainty that this woman's behavior deserves to be measured against the criteria for insanity and that she should not be found wanting, whereas there is such a public outcry against the same standard successfully applied to the case of John W. Hinckley. Mr. Hinckley is no less a sympathetic character: so hopelessly—madly, one might say—in love with a minor actress in a third-rate movie; so much the victim of loneliness, of psychological inadequacy; the central character of a patently bizarre tale. Why should there have been such an outcry against his verdict, such a sense of justice miscarried?

I propose that the outcry has little to do with the merits and liabilities of the insanity defense and much to do with the social importance of the intended victim. Attitudes toward defendants vary considerably as a function of the seriousness of the allegations against them. Although the dictum "Better to let 10 guilty men go free than to convict one innocent man" (Blackstone 4) is widely believed, the number of people whom we are willing to set free depends enormously on the crime in question. With a petty crime, we are quite willing to preserve the integrity of the innocent. But, as the crime becomes more serious, we are less willing to take risks, the desire for retribution becomes more intense, and the number of guilty people whom we are willing to set free in order to spare an innocent one—the guilty/innocent ratio—declines. These findings, from a recent work by Mark Masling (1982), are shown in Table 1. The findings themselves are dramatic: The Spearman rank-difference correlation between mean ratings of crime seriousness and median guilty/innocent ratios is $-.95$, $p<.01$.

As one might expect from these data, the more serious the allegation is, the more willing people are to suspend such due process rights as the exclusionary rule, the right to remain free before trial, and the

Table 1

Median G/I Ratios, and Seriousness Ratings
for Blackstone Study 1: Crimes With Victims

Type of crime	Seriousness ratings	Median G/I ratio
murder	9.98	5
rape	9.45	10
child molestation	8.62	10
airplane hijacking	8.02	10
armed robbery	7.94	10
assault and battery	7.72	13
arson	7.6	10
drunk driving	7.08	15
fraud	5.49	50
vandalism	4.87	35
pickpocket	4.13	50
shoplifting	4.0	50
indecent exposure	3.36	60
cocaine (possession)	2.6	100
marijuana (possession)	1.8	100

Note. Adapted from *Crime Seriousness and Attitudes Towards the Accused* by
M. S. Masling, 1982, Doctoral dissertation, p. 100.

right to avoid direct self-incrimination. That is precisely what Masling
finds. People are much more willing to implement due process for those
who are accused of shoplifting or even burglary, for example, than they
are for those accused of arson or child molesting. Finally, people seem
more willing to convict those accused of serious than those accused of
less serious crimes, even when the type of evidence is identical.

All these data suggest that, as the perceived seriousness of the
crime increases, people become more willing to abandon the ordinary
protections accorded defendants. People seem concerned more with
punishing someone for the crime than with carefully examining whether
the accused person is truly guilty. For this reason, when the victim of an
attempted murder is a significant public figure, as in the Hinckley case,
or when the respondent is someone to whom the victim was significant
(such as the mother of that five-year-old child), there is an understandable and documented tendency to root out the villain and to be upset if
the villain "escapes" on grounds of insanity. Because people do not
understand the relationship between crime seriousness and the desire
for conviction, they are often and puzzlingly of two minds regarding the
insanity defense. Sometimes, as in the Hinckley case, they find that defense unjust and want to see it abolished or at least modified. Yet these
same people will recall other cases in which they were comfortable with

the identical outcome. Discomfort arises as a function of the perceived seriousness of the crime. Everyone recognizes that murder is awful, and no one would dismiss the life of a five-year-old child. Yet, in the order of things, and because a president is psychologically much more than a person, attempts on the life of the president are considered much more awful than many other offenses.

The Burden of Proof of Sanity

Beyond the seriousness of the crime and its relation to the perception of guilt, a further observation can usefully be made about the insanity defense; this observation concerns the determination of *sanity*. Linguistically the positive instances of words carry their meaning, while the negative instances merely negate that meaning. *Tolerance* and *attractiveness*, for example, are meaningful. When I say that someone is intolerant and unattractive, I am simply negating that meaning. But that is not the case for the words *sanity* and *insanity*, any more than it is for such words as *normal* and *abnormal*. There the *negative* instance carries the meaning. We can define *abnormality* and *insanity* more easily than we can their opposites. Indeed, there is good reason to believe that their opposites cannot be defined at all (Rosenhan & Seligman, in press).

In Hinckley's case, the burden fell to the prosecution to prove beyond a reasonable doubt that Hinckley was sane. To prove sanity, however, is simply impossible, not because the standard is too high (Cohen, 1982), as some commentators have suggested, but because sanity cannot be defined in a way that allows such proof (Kaufman, 1982). A competent physician has no hesitancy in diagnosing a particular disease, but which physician can state positively, under oath no less, that someone is perfectly healthy? One cannot prove that someone is sane, regardless of the requisite standard of proof. The federal court requirement that sanity must be proved beyond a reasonable doubt needs to be changed.

The Use of the Insanity Defense

The uninformed observer might feel that the outcry against the insanity defense results from its wide and successful use. This is not so. Recent testimony before Congress by Henry Steadman, as well as ongoing investigations (Steadman, Monahan, Hartstone, Davis, & Robbins, 1982), make clear that the insanity defense is rarely invoked and, when invoked, is frequently unsuccessful. During 1978, for example, only 1,625 persons were admitted to state and federal hospitals throughout the United States after successfully pleading insanity to some crime. That statistic averages to slightly over 30 cases per state per year. The crimes were not uniformly serious. Rather, a substantial proportion of the insanity pleas were entered for relatively minor crimes. Steadman estimates that insanity pleas related to serious crime are entered in fewer than two cases of every thousand felony arrests. In most of these cases there would be near uniform agreement that a successful insanity plea was a just outcome of the trial. The cases that make us question the insanity defense, therefore, arise from a minute proportion of all the criminal trials in the United States and from a minute proportion of all of the insanity pleas.[1]

Expert Testimony and State of Mind

Commentators on the Hinckley trial commonly note, often with dismay if not contempt, that seven psychiatrists offered testimony in the trial and nearly all of the testimony was conflicting. The state of psychological knowledge is such, they say, that even its most eminent authorities cannot agree whether Hinckley was sane or insane in a strictly legal sense.

In a strictly legal sense what does it mean to be sane? The standard in the federal court in which Hinckley was tried (attempts on the lives of public officials are considered federal offenses) is as follows:

> A person is not responsible for criminal conduct if at the time of such conduct as a result of mental disease or defect he lacks substantial capacity either to appreciate the criminality of his conduct or to conform his conduct to the requirements of law. (ALI Model Penal Code, 1962)

This rule is used in 30 states as well as in the federal courts.[2]

---

[1]My colleague Robert Mnookin (Note 1) points out, rightly in my view, that these carefully gleaned statistics may convey an erroneous impression because, even with the insanity defense, there is always bargaining in the shadow of the law—which is to say, that the insanity defense, like any other, is used in plea bargaining.

[2]The remaining states, in the main, use the M'Naghten Rule, which interestingly developed from circumstances quite similar to those enveloping John Hinckley. Daniel M'Naghten suffered from what today would be called delusions of persecution. He considered his major persecutor to be Robert Peel, prime minister of England during the early years of Victoria's reign. M'Naghten came to London intent on killing Peel and would have succeeded had Peel not decided to ride with the queen that day. Peel's secretary, Drummond, riding in the carriage that would normally have been occupied by Peel, was killed.

After a lengthy trial in 1843, M'Naghten was found not guilty by reason of insanity. His counsel relied extensively on Dr. Isaac Ray's *Medical Jurisprudence of Insanity*, published in 1838. In that book Ray pointed out the weaknesses of the right–wrong tests that had been used until that time and suggested that not only knowledge but the ability to control one's behavior is relevant to whether one's acts should be construed as criminal. The lord

From the viewpoint of law, guilt is determined by one's state of mind and not alone by one's behavior. State of mind is not an easy matter to determine. First, the law requires a retrospective analysis, an assessment of the defendant's mental state—not as it is today but as it was when the act was committed.

Second, the law requires a determination of whether the defendant was able to appreciate the criminality of his conduct—not merely to know whether what he or she did was wrong but to appreciate its wrongfulness, to have an emotional response to that knowledge (cf. Livermore & Meehl, 1967). Appreciation is more difficult to define and assess than is knowledge; but because the stakes are high, the additional effort is warranted.

Third, the rule mandates an assessment of whether the defendant was able to conform his or her conduct to the requirements of law. That assessment is especially difficult, for it requires the expert witness to distinguish between being *unable* to control one's behavior and being *unwilling* to do so.

These legal tasks necessitate quite a bit in terms of psychological theory and research. The first task—assessing the state of mind at the time of an act that may have occurred months ago—requires deep understanding of the relations between the past and the present and of the durability of mental states and requires the ability of psychologists and psychiatrists to distinguish the simulated from the real. The second task taxes us even further, for it requires not merely a test of knowledge (we do fairly well with those) but a test of appreciation and understanding. "Mere intellectual awareness that conduct is wrongful, when divorced from appreciation or understanding of the moral or legal import of behavior, can have little significance" (*U.S. v. Freeman,* 1966).

chief justice was so impressed with these arguments that he practically directed the verdict of not guilty by reason of insanity.

Neither the prime minister nor the queen (on whose life there had already been three attempts) was pleased; both pressed the House of Lords to consider the law on criminal responsibility. In an environment of considerable pressure and hysteria, not unlike the environment surrounding today's debate, the 15 judges of the common law court examined the matter and, led by the same lord chief justice who had been so impressed with Isaac Ray's work, reversed that view and enunciated the following, much narrower one.

[I]t must be clearly proved that, at the time of the committing of the act, the party accused was labouring under such a defect of reason, from disease of the mind, as not to know the nature and quality of the act he was doing; or, if he did know it, that he did not know he was doing what was wrong.

Had Daniel M'Naghten been tried under the rule that is named for him, he would have been found guilty. Such are the consequences of changing laws under high emotion. Isaac Ray's important understandings about criminality were lost to the courts (except those in New Hampshire, where the enlightened insanity rule held sway) for more than a century.

Finally, the rule asks that we distinguish between voluntary and involuntary behavior. That request is particularly formidable, as that remarkable English critic, Lady Wootton, observed:

> [I]f I assert that I have an uncontrollable impulse to break shop windows, in the nature of the case no proof of uncontrollability can be adduced. All that is known is that the impulse was not in fact controlled; and it is perfectly legitimate to hold the opinion that, had I tried a little harder, I might have conquered it. (Wootton, 1968, 1026–1027)

Fortunately, as this discussion shows, we are not required to bring absolute proof on this matter, merely evidence that supports the view that the behavior was involuntary.

Beyond all this, the rule levies one final tax on our acumen: to determine if the failure to appreciate criminality or to control one's impulses was the result of mental disease or defect. This is a heavy burden on knowledge, for there is considerable evidence that the assessment of mental disease or defect is not a highly reliable procedure under the best of circumstances (Ennis & Litwack, 1974; Morse, 1978; Rosenhan, 1973, 1975; but see Spitzer, 1975, for a critique of this position). But even if determining mental disease were easy, we are asked to go a step further and to assess whether difficulties in appreciation and conformance *arose* from the alleged disease. This is a considerably more difficult matter.

These tasks exceed our abilities, often substantially; psychological science is not advanced sufficiently to address these matters with certainty. Quite properly we undertake these tasks with considerable humility; and our findings are not yet God-given truths but reflect only our best judgments. In the courtroom we offer expert testimony not because our views are God-given but because our knowledge about these matters exceeds that of laymen and will probably aid the trier in the search for truth. If our knowledge is not yet perfect, neither is it trivial or useless.

Forensic Psychologists and Psychiatrists

No discussion of expert testimony can be complete without a word about the experts themselves; in that area the news is variable. The American Board of Forensic Psychology (ABFP) each year examines a substantial number of those who practice psychology in the legal arena. Some are social, experimental, or industrial psychologists who lend their skills to legal issues. But the largest group is psychologists who were trained and certified in the clinical and counseling areas and who are involved in such matters as determining competency to stand trial, assessing the mental state at the time of the crime, advising in civil commitments and divorce negotiations, determining child custody, and treating those who have been committed to psychiatric hospitals, particularly the criminally insane. The testimony of these psychologists is crucial in determining the fate of thousands of people. Their efforts touch on many more lives than the typical clinician. How well do they fare?

To the extent that its examinations are valid assessments of actual performance in the legal arena, the board has tested some brilliant candidates: knowledgeable, judicious, thoughtful, sensible, infused with remarkably good judgment. In such examinations, the candidates have been able to distinguish best guess from hard fact and to demonstrate well-honed skills in the forensic area. Those skills are by no means identical to the skills of a good clinical psychologist. The context of the forensic inquiry, the kinds of questions that are asked, the use to which information will be put, not to speak of the legal knowledge that is required, all serve to distinguish forensic clinical psychology from clinical psychology itself. Not uncommonly, people who hold diplomas in clinical psychology fail the forensic examination. One of the most common reasons for failing is the candidate's inability to recognize the unique features of forensic practice, its special requirements, and its special skills (Howell, Jackson, Rosenhan, & Weissman, in press).

Finally, in assessing the utility of expert testimony from mental health professionals, as in other kinds of assessments, comparison groups are useful. My own sense that psychologists and psychiatrists have much to offer the courts arises from my courtroom observations of experts from other disciplines. For example, economists often testify in antitrust litigation on the definition of market share and on an evaluation of a share of the market sufficiently large to make a firm a just target for antitrust litigation. The issues are complex; it is a rare case that does not have economists lined up on both sides of the litigation. Similar observations could be made with regard to negligence and the host of issues that arise in tort law and require the testimony of experts. Those who have witnessed a personal injury case of any magnitude have observed qualified experts—orthopedists, engineers, nephrologists, metallurgists, oncologists, and photographers—arrayed on both sides of the case. Wherever there is some ambiguity about the nature of an occurrence, there will be dispute. Expert testimony does not resolve dispute; it merely illuminates each party's interest.

Child Custody

The theoretical and empirical shortcomings of psychology are most evident when psychology is called on to decide custody of a child. Divorce is a splendid solution for adults and a disaster for children (Hetherington, Cox, & Cox, 1978; Hetherington, Cox, & Cox, 1979; Wallerstein & Kelly, 1980). Some of the troubling issues in determining custody are illuminated in a recent paper by Beaber (Note 2), who asks us to imagine that we have completed a psychological assessment of a family that is being dissolved. The relevant findings from this assessment are that neither parent suffers severe psychopathology, neither is utterly incompetent to parent. More commonly, both meet the minimal standards for being a parent. The court requires help to decide who will be the *better* parent.

Let us imagine that a psychologist has testified that the mother of a seven-year-old boy is hostile and rejecting and views her son as a symbolic equivalent of her husband, whom she hates and chose to divorce. The psychologist predicts that she would subject the child to endless rejection experiences and would produce severe damage to his self-esteem. The best guess an experienced forensic psychologist makes is that there would be irreparable damage to this boy. During the cross-examination, the attorney for the other side presents the following line of questioning:

> Doctor, imagine if you will, that this rejection by the mother causes the child to have, indeed, very low self-esteem. Soon this child would become extremely insecure and would seek out the approval of other females in his environment. Assume further, doctor, that the child executed that particular psychodynamic by seeking out the approval of all his female teachers, and to a lesser extent, male teachers. Assume, as a result of having this pathological need for correcting the painful derogating self-esteem experience with his mother, that he studied unusually hard and became unusually precocious with regard to certain subject matters. Assume, doctor, just for a moment, that one of those teachers—a biology teacher—was a female who had an unusual similarity to his mother. Assume this teacher had a high standard of conduct and was very critical. Assume further that this child was unusually gifted and he constantly tried to symbolically correct that emotional trauma of this childhood by struggling harder and harder. Assume that child went to medical school. Assume that his neurosis ultimately caused that child to feel the need to do something of overwhelming significance for the population of the world. Assume that child eventually won the Nobel prize for inventing a new antibiotic and that millions of people who would have otherwise died of some medical complication or disease would now survive. Assume as a result of that, that at age 30, he would be rich, wealthy and famous. Assume women on the faculty of medical school, students throughout the school, people who came in contact with him, loved and adored him—giving him that adoration that he never had as a child and giving him a sense of self-esteem, and narcissism to more than compensate for

the damage done by his mother. Assume that all those things were true, doctor, would you still form the opinion that it is in the best interest of that child not to be with his mother? (Beaber, 1982, pp. 2–3)

This hypothetical example, much overdrawn but illustrative, raises serious questions about the ability to predict and about the role of chance (cf. Bandura, 1982). In another paper in this book, John Monahan deals directly with the ability of social scientists to predict one particularly significant social behavior, violence. In the present context it is important to underscore that the problems of prediction addressed by Monahan (cf. Monahan, 1981) are associated not merely with violence but with many other areas of behavior. In the preceding custody decision, how this boy will grow up and what he will endure in the process depend on many things that seem quite beyond prediction. The child's welfare will be affected by whether his mother remarries and, if she does, by whom she remarries and by how well the husband gets along with the child; by how well the child likes and gets along with the husband; by whether the new couple has other children; by how all of the children are viewed by their parents; by how the natural father reacts to all of this—one could continue endlessly.

Although there is not yet one reliable follow-up study of custody decisions and placements (there is one promising study underway by Michael Wald, Merrill Carlsmith, and Herbert Leiderman), we commonly assume that some monotonic relationship exists between the way that we assess a parent-child relationship at the present time and how that relationship will ultimately affect a child. No such monotonic relationship exists. Thus fortuity in human affairs weakens our prophecies and renders us, if we have any sense at all, modest in our predictions about human endeavor.

The Duty to Protect

Mental health professionals construe their relationship with clients as a private one that exists nearly in vacuo and imposes on the professional one and only one obligation: to help the client. That construction has been vastly revised in the 1970s, and nothing has revised it more than the *Tarasoff* decisions (1974, 1976). In the second of those two decisions, the California Supreme Court held that "[w]hen a therapist determines, or pursuant to the standards of his profession should determine, that his patient presents a serious danger of violence to another, he incurs an obligation to use reasonable care to protect the intended victim against such danger." The issues in *Tarasoff* have been widely misunderstood by mental health professionals, and it will be useful first to review the case.

Prosenjit Poddar, a member of the Indian "untouchable" caste, was a student of naval architecture at the University of California at Berkeley. At folk dancing classes he met and fell in love with Tatiana Tarasoff. She, however, spurned his affections and apparently as a result, he became depressed and sought treatment as a voluntary psychiatric out-patient at the Cowell Student Health Clinic. He informed his therapist that he was going to kill a girl when she returned from her vacation in Brazil, and although Poddar did not name her, the court found that she was readily identifiable as Tatiana Tarasoff. The psychologist notified the police and recommended emergency commitment and observation. Poddar was briefly confined, and then released because he seemed rational and promised to stay away from Tarasoff. He did not return to treatment after his release, nor was he required to do so. Two months later, after she returned from Brazil, Poddar went to Tatiana's home and killed her with a butcher knife. Poddar was originally convicted of second degree murder. That conviction was reversed for judicial failure to give adequate instructions concerning a defense of diminished capacity. He was later convicted of voluntary manslaughter. According to one writer, he is now back in India and happily married. (Stone, 1976, p. 358)

Tarasoff's parents brought suit against several defendants, including the Cowell therapists, for failure to warn Tatiana or her parents of Poddar's threats. The California Supreme Court found that the plaintiffs had a valid cause of action for negligent failure to warn.

As a general rule a person has *absolutely no duty* to control the conduct of another (*Richards v. Stanley*, 1954) or to warn those endangered by such conduct (*Restatement 2d Torts*, 1965). For example, an expert swimmer who has a boat and rope nearby and sees someone drowning may sit on the dock, smoke a cigarette, and watch the person drown—with no fear of subsequent legal consequences (*Osterlind v. Hill*, 1968). No duty to rescue exists even where one incites an acquaintance to jump into the water and then lets him or her drown (*Yania v. Bigan*, 1959). Again, one has no obligation to rescue a child who is drowning in a swimming pool (*Handiboe v. McCarthy*, 1966). Prosser, the preeminent authority in such matters, bluntly states that "the law has persistently refused to recognize the moral obligation of common decency and common humanity, to come to the aid of another human being who is in danger, even though the outcome is to cost him his life" (Prosser, 1971, p. 340).

On what basis could *Tarasoff* be pursued? Although the general rule applies quite broadly, the courts have carved out several exceptions. One exception occurs when a special relationship between two people gives one person the right to expect protection from the other (Prosser,

1971, 340). Historically this category has included such relationships as carrier and passenger, innkeeper and guest, school district and pupil, employer and employee, and landlord and tenant (Harper & Kime, 1933–1934). In other cases, courts have found a parental duty to warn a hired baby-sitter of the violent propensities of a child (*Ellis v. D'Angelo,* 1953) and a state duty to warn foster parents of the dangerous propensities of its ward (*Johnson v. State,* 1968). But these cases obviously do not control the court's finding because in *Tarasoff* there was no direct relationship between the therapist and Poddar's victim. Moreover, special knowledge, which is the basis for the imposition of a duty to warn in these cases, is arguably absent in *Tarasoff,* because mental health professionals predict violent behaviors quite poorly (see Monahan, this volume).

Other duties arise from the special relationship between two persons in which one of them controls the other's behavior. In such cases a special relationship between the defendant and the victim is not necessary if the defendant was (or should have been) in control of the person whose conduct posed the danger. Thus the duty of a hospital staff to exercise reasonable care to protect suicidal patients against foreseeable harm is well-established.[3] Similarly, a hospital that releases a patient negligently[4] or fails to exercise proper control over a patient (*Greenberg v. Barbour,* 1971) is liable for that patient's actions.

But even this line of cases—many of which were cited in *Tarasoff*—does not justify imposing a duty to warn on psychotherapists because private practitioners, unlike hospitals, have neither the right nor the ability to restrain and control their patients. In *Bellah v. Greenson* the court recognized this important difference: "Obviously, the duty imposed upon those responsible for the care of a patient in an institutional setting differs from that which may be involved in the case of a psychiatrist treating patients on an outpatient basis" (*Bellah v. Greenson,* 1978).

The imposition of a duty in the absence of a corresponding ability (or right) to control creates an obviously unworkable situation for

[3]*Bornmann v. Great Southwest General Hospital, Inc.,* 453 F. 2d 616, 621 (5th Cir. 1971);*Peitrucha v. Grant Hospital,* 447 F. 2d 1029, 1033 (7th Cir. 1971);*Dinnerstein v. United States,* 486 F. 2d 34, 36–37 (2d Cir. 1973);*Stuppy v. United States,* 560 F. 2d 373, 375 (8th Cir. 1977); *Abille v. United States,* 482 F. Supp. 703 (N.D. Cal 1984).
[4]Cf. *Williams v. United States,* 450 F. Supp. 1040 (D.S.D. 1978). In this case, a Veterans Administration hospital was held liable for the death of a person killed by a patient who was released by the hospital, although the patient's violent tendencies were known to the hospital. In *Merchants National Bank & Trust Co. v. United States,* 272 F. Supp. 409 (D.N.D. 1967), it was held that a hospital had not exercised proper care in releasing a patient who had threatened to kill his wife and did so upon his release.

psychotherapists.[5] Nevertheless, the Tarasoff court, citing Prosser, felt that neither the absence of precedent nor the difficulties of imposing control were crippling because duty "is not sacrosanct in itself, but only an expression of the sum total of those considerations of policy which led the law to say that the particular plaintiff is entitled to protection" (*Tarasoff v. Regents*, 1964, supra n. 16, pp. 332–333).

The Parameters of Tarasoff

Before examining the nature of that duty, noting the parameters of the *Tarasoff* duty may be useful. First, *Tarasoff* has been applied outside California. In *McIntosh v. Milano* (1979) a wrongful death action was brought against a psychiatrist whose patient murdered the plaintiff's daughter. The patient had related violent fantasies to his therapist and communicated a desire to make other people fear him. He displayed a knife during therapy sessions and told of firing a BB gun at the victim's car and windows. Another psychiatrist testified at the trial that the defendant's conduct had constituted a gross deviation from accepted medical practice by failing to protect the decedent. The court held that the defendant had a duty to take whatever steps were necessary to protect the potential victim. Courts in Florida and in Nebraska have similarly held with *Tarasoff* (*Department of Health and Rehabilitative Services v. McDougall*, 1978; *Lipari v. Sears, Roebuck & Company*, 1980). But in *Case v. United States* (1981), the court refused to extend *Tarasoff* to Ohio, noting that "*Tarasoff* stands almost alone in its holding."

Second, the therapist's duty under *Tarasoff* does not extend to unknown victims or even to a narrow class of potential victims. In a recent case a county was sued for negligently releasing a juvenile delinquent from custody although he had indicated that, if released, he would kill a child in the neighborhood. Shortly after release he sexually assaulted and murdered the plaintiff's son. But the California Supreme Court rejected the plaintiff's contention that they had a valid cause of action,

[5]There is only one case where a duty was imposed in the absence of either a direct relationship with the victim or control over the tortfeasor. In *Simonsen v. Swenson* (104 Neb. 224,177 N.W. 831 [1920]), a physician correctly diagnosed syphilis, warned the patient that it was contagious, and asked him to leave his hotel accommodations and to enter a period of physical isolation. When the patient refused, the doctor warned the hotel manager, who evicted the patient. The Nebraska Supreme Court, in holding for the doctor in a breach of confidence suit, recognized the doctor's duty to those who might have been endangered. "No patient can expect that if his malady is found to be a dangerously contagious nature he can still require it to be kept secret from those to whom . . . such diseases would be transmitted" (p. 832). But *Simonsen*, of course, is quite distinct from *Tarasoff*. *Simonsen* sued for breach of confidence. The Court does not indicate whether the physician would have been liable had he remained silent. Beyond the nature of the suit itself, the diagnosis of syphillis in 1920 was far more accurate than the prediction of violence is today.

emphasizing that when an individual poses a risk to a significant portion of the community, there is no duty to warn because the value of such warnings is not great and because such warnings are a severe burden to public agencies.[6]

Finally, in *Bellah* (1977) the Court refused to extend *Tarasoff* to self-inflicted harm or suicide.

This quick overview of the obligations imposed by *Tarasoff* leaves the question that is commonly raised in this context: Under what conditions, and how well, can dangerous behavior be predicted? I provide no answers to that question but recommend the paper by John Monahan in this volume.

Instead, I want to turn to a different issue, one that is very much part of *Tarasoff* and part of the many other issues where law and treatment join. It is often alleged that the *Tarasoff* rulings have had enormous consequences for treatment (Stone, 1976). Of major concern has been the possibility that these decisions can undermine the therapeutic alliance by making it difficult for patients with aggressive feelings to confide fully in their therapist. There is some evidence that the decisions have made psychotherapists a bit more fearful when issues of violent behavior arise, especially in California, where the *Tarasoff* decisions have binding authority ("Where the Public Peril Begins," 1978). These kinds of concerns raise two issues. First, what is a treatment? Second, what is the appropriate treatment for people who threaten violent acts?

What Is a Treatment?

Some definition of *treatment* is necessary not only in the context of *Tarasoff* but also in regard to the complex issues of the right to treatment and right to refuse treatment. That definition is not so easily obtained. If we define a *crime* as the joint occurrence of an unfortunate act and evil intentions on the part of the actor, then correspondingly we could define a *treatment* as the joint occurrence of a benign professional act and good intentions on the part of the therapist. Unfortunately that is not the common definition of *treatment*. In law and in fact treatment is that which someone calls treatment and nothing more. One need not demonstrate that a putative treatment works or that it is benign in order for it to be called treatment. One need not even require that the professional or institution providing the treatment have benign intentions or any intentions at all. Merely calling it treatment makes it so, Pygmalion-style.

---

[6]27 Cal. 3d 741, 614 P. 2d 728, 167 Cal. Rptr. 70 (1980). See also *Mavroudis v. Superior Court*, 102 Cal. App. 3d 594 (1980); *Hooks v. Southern California Permanente*, 107 Cal. App. 3d 435, 444, 165 Cal. Rptr. 741, 746 (1981). In *Lipari* the hospital *was* held to a duty to protect the public at large, although the hospital was asked to control rather than warn.

The law constantly pricks psychology (and psychiatry) into providing a better and more useful definition of *treatment*. The classic series of cases that began with *Rouse v. Cameron* (1966), continued through the Alabama cases (*Wyatt v. Stickney*, 1971, 1972), and resurfaced recently in *Youngberg v. Romeo*, dealt with precisely that issue: whether what we and our psychiatric colleagues call treatment is really that; whether *hospitalization, custodial treatment, and milieu treatment*, to name but a few, qualify as treatment in any meaningful sense of that word. The law has insisted that there must be more than label. Treatment for Mr. Romeo, the Supreme Court recently wrote, would require at least minimally adequate habilitation training. Although the Court has been reluctant to enunciate any *constitutional* right to particular kinds of treatment, it has been offended by the notion that one can do little more than hospitalize a person and call that treatment. A nonlawyer observer such as myself might well conclude that fewer such cases would come to the Supreme Court had we been clearer about what is meant by treatment in the first place.

This discussion of the meaning of treatment in a variety of classic right-to-treatment cases is no digression from the topic at hand, the impact of *Tarasoff*. Although the impact of *Tarasoff* on treatment has been a focal topic of concern, *treatment* has never been explicitly defined. Nearly uniformly, the various writings imply that treatment of violent intentions is defined by the therapist's intentions alone and not by the therapeutic outcome. Indeed, if treatment were judged by the *outcome*, I question whether the treatment of Prosenjit Poddar would qualify. My own recent review of the literature located no evidence that outpatient treatment of the traditional, insight-oriented, one-on-one variety reduces the probability of subsequent violent behavior. The psychologist who saw Poddar apparently thought the same thing: He recommended that Poddar be hospitalized.[7]

What Treatments Work?

Tarasoff tacitly pricks psychology to examine what it means in calling a procedure a *treatment*. For example, a woman comes to a psychologist with a headful of murderous fantasies, all directed at her husband. Would the psychologist treat that woman individually? One would not if questioning revealed that her husband had been beating her. Or a man comes to a psychologist with a headful of murderous fantasies, all directed at his wife. An inquiry convinces the psychologist that the wife is involved in multiple, indiscreet, extramarital affairs. Would the psychologist treat that man individually or try to involve the spouse?

[7]The psychologist was not recommending hospitalization primarily as treatment but rather because he felt that Poddar was dangerous to another person. Because the psychologist's own ministrations were not availing, hospitalization was recommended to protect others.

Angry and aggressive impulses are fundamentally *social* impulses, which are best treated in a *social* context. The most illuminating psychological analyses of aggression reveal it to be an interpersonal impulse that is overwhelmingly cued by external events and situational cognitions, rather than by traits (Bandura, 1973; Patterson, 1976). Moreover, the available sociological evidence indicates that most angry people are angry at people about whom they care, and most violence is done on intimates. The combination of data suggests that one-on-one insight-oriented therapy will rarely be the treatment of choice for problems of violence.[8] As David Wexler (1979) observes, one of the virtues of the *Tarasoff* decision may be that it reminds us that intended victims quite often play an active role in the passions generated in violence-threatening persons.[9]

Social and Political Abuse of Abnormal Psychology

Clinical psychology and psychiatry aim to help people. However, in various societies at various times, these professions have been used toward political ends. In order to confine or control individuals who hold dissident views, political leaders have often sanctioned abuses of personal liberties in the name of psychiatry and psychology. In large part the potential for abuse rises from the definitional vaguenesses of psychological abnormality and the difficulties of determining legal insanity. Whether people are seen as abnormal depends on whether they possess a family resemblance to other abnormal people (Rosenhan & Seligman, in press).

There need not be a perfect match between the behaviors of those people and the behaviors of abnormal people: As long as *some* elements are similar, individuals might be considered abnormal by society. Among those behaviors or elements of abnormality are whether the person produces discomfort in others; the degree to which the behavior is unconventional, and the degree to which the behavior violates idealized standards. If an individual's behavior triggers these criteria, that person may be labeled abnormal even though other criteria of abnormality, such as intense suffering, are absent.

---

[8]Incidentally, for violent impulses that appear to have no specific target—nonspecific, diffuse anger—there is no duty to protect. The duty to protect emerges only when there is a readily identifiable target of violence.

[9]In the imaginary scenario wherein Hinckley undergoes treatment for his dangerous impulses (that is, before his attempt on President Reagan's life), it would not be possible to ask Reagan to participate. Nevertheless, it is hard to resist speculating about the source of Hinckley's anger. News reports lead me to infer that Hinckley was a very lonely and uprooted man. If that inference were correct, a social therapy, designed to enable him to overcome his loneliness and to enable him to find roots, would be called for.

Thus it is not unlikely that people who hold different views from those of a society's leaders might be seen (or made to be seen) as unconventional or in violation of idealized standards. It is therefore easy to consider them abnormal, to overlook the fact that they fail to meet any of the other criteria for abnormality, and to bend that perceived abnormality to meet the legal definition of insanity.

Beyond the potential abuse that relies on the definitional ambiguities of abnormality, abuse arises from the fact that the meanings of abnormality change dramatically over time. In DSM-II, which was approved by the American Psychiatric Association in 1968, homosexuality was listed as a mental disorder. New information revealed that as much as 10 percent of the adult population practices homosexuality. The behavior, therefore, was no longer as unconventional as it had seemed, nor did it violate community standards as intensely as earlier. Consequently, in 1976, by a vote of its membership, the association decided that homosexuality was no longer a psychiatric disorder. Homosexuality was cured by that single vote. Similarly, in 1966, the American Association for Mental Deficiency reduced the IQ required for designating a person mentally retarded from 80 to 70, thereby releasing more than a million people from the retarded category.

Attitudes toward work, sexuality, manners, the opposite sex, marriage, clothing—indeed, toward most of the significant aspects of social life—have changed over the decades and continue to change. Canons of appropriate behavior and attitude, which are fundamental to judgments of normality and abnormality, change too. What might have been considered abnormal even a decade ago is presently considered normal; correspondingly, some behaviors that might be viewed as normal today could be viewed as abnormal in a few years.

Potential for abuse arises also from the enormous power with which society endows psychologists and psychiatrists. Perry London (1964) calls them a "secular priesthood"; Thomas Szasz (1970) sees (and decries) the rise of the "therapeutic state." Any reservations that people might have about psychiatry and psychology often dissolve when their own lives are touched by psychological distress. Such people tend to accept the views of experts. Their personal reliance on a practitioner and their vulnerability to the practitioner's judgments and recommendations make all clients of psychiatry and psychology particularly vulnerable to abuse. In general two kinds of abuse can be distinguished: abuse by the state and abuse by society.

Abuse by the State

Psychiatric diagnosis and subsequent involuntary hospitalization are widely used to stifle political dissent. During the 1970s particularly, widespread reliance on political psychiatry by the government of the

Soviet Union has been revealed. At least 210 cases of *sane* people who were interned in Soviet prison-hospitals for political reasons have been reported (Bloch & Reddaway, 1977). Others claim even higher figures (see A. Podrabenek in Fireside, 1979).

How is this done, particularly in the Soviet Union, where the legal safeguards against abuse of involuntary commitment procedures are clearly stronger than in many other countries? Soviet law, for example, allows the individual's family to nominate one or more psychiatrists to the examining commission; it requires that the family be notified of the results of the examination; and it states that an individual cannot be held for more than three days for purposes of examination. Nevertheless, these rules can be circumvented, as the experience of the Russian scientist, Zhores A. Medvedev, indicates.

Medvedev is a talented biologist whose interests range the gamut from medical gerontology to the sociology and history of science. One of his manuscripts was confiscated by the Soviet secret police during a search of a colleague's apartment. There was nothing illegal about the manuscript, but it had been found amid a group of "samizdat," or underground publications. Medvedev, moreover, was known to be an outspoken scientist, who had been in "trouble" before. In fact, he had been unemployed for more than a year, having been relieved from his post in the Institute of Medical Radiology.

Medvedev was deceived into a psychiatric interview, which was conducted under the guise of discussing his son. Subsequently, two psychiatrists as well as several police arrived at his home. Medvedev was again interviewed, now under quite strained conditions, and then forcibly removed to the local psychiatric hospital. He was seen subsequently by several other psychiatrists. Despite all the stress he underwent, he must generally have appeared quite robust to them, for the worst they could say was that he had a "psychopathic personality" (the Soviet term for neurotic), "an exaggerated opinion of himself" and was "poorly adapted to his social environment." They noted that his writing in recent years was weaker than his earlier work, and observed as a further symptom that Medvedev had shown "'excessively scrupulous' attention to detail in his general writings." (see Medvedev & Medvedev, 1979)

Medvedev was held for 19 days, a relatively brief time for these proceedings, and then released. But another outspoken Russian, Pyotr Grigorenko, suffered a worse fate. Grigorenko was a distinguished general who had served in the Red Army for 35 years. At the age of 54, he began to question the policies of the Communist Party of which he was a member. Ultimately, he was sent for psychiatric examination at Moscow's Serbsky Institute, where his diagnosis was "Paranoid development of the personality, with reformist ideas arising in the personality, with psychopathic features of the character, and the presence of symptoms of arteriosclerosis of the brain." Shortly thereafter, he underwent an examination by a second group of psychiatrists who found him admirably sane and vigorous. But a third commission overruled the second, and as a result, Grigorenko spent six years in three of the most difficult Soviet "psychoprisons" before he was permitted to emigrate to the United States. (see Fireside, 1979)

Although some of the psychiatrists who examined Medvedev and Grigorenko may consciously have subverted scientific knowledge to political expediency, many probably did not. Rather, they were well-known and highly regarded psychiatrists, both within and outside the Soviet Union, who *truly believed* that these people were ill. These psychiatrists would point out that one symptom of these people's illness— and not, by any means, the only one—was their unconventionality, which consisted in their openly questioning and occasionally defying the system.

The unwitting use of psychology and psychiatry for political ends is widespread and not a practice confined to the Soviet Union. For example, after the Second World War, Ezra Pound, the eminent poet, was taken into custody by the American troops in Italy, returned to the United States, and charged with treason. Pound had lived in Fascist Italy during the war and had supported Mussolini. The broadcasts that Pound made from Rome were alleged to be treasonous. Pound denied the charge but never came to trial. Instead, the government and his attorneys agreed that he was incompetent to stand trial. He was therefore remanded to St. Elizabeth's Hospital in Washington, D.C., and effectively imprisoned without trial. Thirteen years later, in 1958, he was still considered incurably insane but not dangerous to others; he was therefore released.

Throughout his life Pound had been an eccentric: enormously conceited, flamboyant, sometimes downright outrageous. Yet he had never brushed with the law, nor had he ever been remanded for psychiatric care. But because his politics were aversive, his eccentricities were invoked to indicate that he was not of sane mind and therefore could not stand trial. Conceit and flamboyance became "grandiosity of ideas and beliefs" and contributed to the diagnostic impression that he was of unsound mind.

Abuse of psychology and psychiatry by the state commonly occurs unconsciously, when the state feels threatened by the actions of the individual and is either unable or unwilling to deal with that threat directly. In many instances fear promotes the state's abuse. And it is fear that underlies individual and social abuse.

Abuse by Society

During the 1972 presidential campaign, George McGovern, the front-running Democratic nominee, proposed Senator Thomas Eagleton as his vice presidential running mate. Eagleton, however, had apparently neglected to tell McGovern that he had been treated for depression, either because he viewed that as private matter or because he feared that the stigma of such treatment might deprive him of the candidacy. If the latter, he was right. The press soon learned that Eagleton had undergone treatment and made a national story of it. After much pressure, McGovern removed him from the ticket. There was no question about Eagleton's effectiveness: He had served, and continues to serve, splendidly as the senator from Missouri. Rather, there was considerable fear that he would weaken the ticket. He was, after all, stigmatized.

Society often stigmatizes people who have sought psychiatric care, frequently to the disadvantage of both the individual and society, as the following case indicates.

Myra Grossman had had a difficult childhood and adolescence. Yet she managed to survive well enough to graduate high school, enter college and be at the very top of her class during her first two years. Conflicts with her parents, however, and a nagging depression, continued unabated and, during her third year, she left school to seek treatment. She began seeing a psychotherapist and subsequently entered a private psychiatric hospital. During that year of treatment, Myra developed considerable ability to deal with her own distress and her family conflicts. She returned to college, continued to major in both chemistry and psychology, earned her Phi Beta Kappa in her junior year and graduated *magna cum laude.*

During her senior year, she applied to medical school. Her Medical College Aptitude Test (MCAT) scores were extraordinarily high and she won a New York State Regents Medical Scholarship. But she was rejected by all thirteen of the schools to which she had applied.

She consulted an attorney and jointly they decided to concentrate on the "easiest" school that had rejected her. Fewer than eight percent of those admitted to this school had won the Regent's Medical Scholarship, none had been admitted to Phi Beta Kappa, and Myra had possibly had the highest MCAT scores of any applicant. She was an attractive person, obviously well motivated, clearly bright. Why then had she been rejected? Clearly it was because of her prior psychiatric hospitalization.

Ms. Grossman and her attorney marshalled clear evidence that she was quite well integrated psychologically. Five psychiatrists and a psychologist testified in effect that she was the better for her prior troubles, and that they had little doubt that she could successfully complete medical school and become a first-rate doctor. She and her attorney successfully demolished the contention that she might still suffer from her prior "illness." But still, the judge ruled against her. Ms. Grossman might have appealed that decision, and might well have won her appeal, had not a far better medical school admitted her and mooted her case (see Ennis, 1972).

The experiences of Zhores Medvedev, Ezra Pound, Pyotr Grigorenko,

Senator Eagleton, and Myra Grossman speak loudly and painfully for themselves. To the extent that judgments of abnormality are social judgments, probably such abuses can never be wholly avoided. But to the extent that psychology and psychiatry remain open and democratic professions that strive for scientifically precise judgments of personality, those dangers surely can be mitigated.

Summary

I began this essay with some observations on the rich diversity of issues and evidence that has been spawned by the union of psychology and law. Even in the relatively narrow area of psychological abnormality and the law, that diversity is so rich as to defy easy summary. I will therefore not attempt a summary except to repeat that the uneasy union between psychology and law holds considerable promise for changing psychology. Regardless of its other virtues, that is reason enough for the union.

Reference Notes

1. Mnookin, R. Personal Communication.
2. Beaber, R. J. *Custody-Quagmire: Some psycho-philosophic dilemmas.* Unpublished manuscript, UCLA Division of Family Medicine, 1982.

References

American Psychiatric Association. *Diagnostic and statistical manual of mental disorders* (2nd ed.). Washington, D.C.: Author, 1968.
Anderson, J., & Bower, G. H. *Human associative memory.* Hillsdale, N.J.: Erlbaum, 1973.
Bandura, A. *Aggression: A social learning analysis.* Englewood Cliffs, N.J.: Prentice-Hall.
Bandura, A. The psychology of chance encounters and life paths. *American Psychologist,* 1982, *37,* 747–755.
Bellah v. Greenson, 73 Cal. App. 3d at 916, 141 Cal. Rptr. 92 at 95 (1977).
Bellah v. Greenson, 81 Cal. Rptr. 3d 614 at 620, 146 Cal. Rptr. 535 at 538 (1978).
Blackstone, W. *Commentaries, 4,* 358.
Bloch, S., & Reddaway, P. *Psychiatric terror: How Soviet psychiatry is used to suppress dissent.* New York: Basic Books, 1977.
Bower, G. H. Mood and memory. *American Psychologist,* 1981, *36,* 129–148.
Case v. United States, 523 F. Supp. 317 (S.D. Ohio 1981).
Cohen, S. It's a mad, mad verdict. *The New Republic,* 1982, *187*(2), 13–16.
Department of Health and Rehabilitative Services v. McDougall, 359 F. 2d 528 (Fla. App. 1978).
Ellis v. D'Angelo, 116 Cal. App. 2d 310, 253 P. 2d 675 (1953).
Ennis, B. J. *Prisoners of psychiatry: Mental patients, psychiatrists, and the law.* New York: Harcourt Brace Jovanovich, 1972.
Ennis, B. J., & Litwack, T. R. Psychiatry and the presumption of expertise: Flipping coins in the courtroom. *California Law Review,* 1974, *62,* 693–752.
Fireside, H. *Soviet psychoprisons.* New York: Norton, 1979.
Greenberg v. Barbour, 322 F. Supp. 745 (E.D. Pa. 1971).

Handiboe v. McCarthy, 114 Ga. App. 541, 151 S.E. 2d 905 (1966).

Harper, F. V., & Kime, P. M. The duty to control the conduct of another. *Yale Law Journal,* 1933–1934, *43,* 886, 898–901.

Hetherington, E. M., Cox, M., & Cox, R. The aftermath of divorce. In J. H. Stevens & M. M. Mathews (Eds.), *Mother-child, father-child relations.* Washington, D.C.: National Association for the Education of Young Children, 1978.

Hetherington, E. M., Cox, M., & Cox, R. Play and social interaction of children following divorce. *Journal of Social Issues,* 1979, 35, 26–49.

Howell, R. J., Jackson, N., Rosenhan, D., & Weissman, H. *Sources of difficulty on American Board of Forensic Psychology examinations,* in press.

Invited testimony before the Subcommittee on Criminal Justice, Committee on the Judiciary, United States House of Representatives, 97th Cong., 2d Sess. (1982).

Johnson v. State, 69 Cal. 2d 782, 447 P. 2d 352, 73 Cal. Rptr. 240 (1968).

Kaufman, I. R. The insanity plea on trial. *The New York Times Magazine,* August 8, 1982, pp. 16–20.

Lipari v. Sears, Roebuck & Company, 497 F. Supp. 185, 194–95 (D. Neb. 1980).

Livermore, J. M., & Meehl, P. E. The virtues of M'Naghten. *Minnesota Law Review,* 1967, *51*(89), 833–855.

London, P. *The modes and morals of psychotherapy.* New York: Holt, Rinehart & Winston, 1964.

Masling, M. S. *Crime seriousness and attitudes towards the accused.* Doctoral dissertation, Stanford University, 1982.

McIntosh v. Milano, 168 N.J. Super. 466, 403 A. 2d 500 (1979).

Medvedev, Z. A., & Medvedev, R. A. *A question of madness.* New York: Norton, 1979.

Meyers, C. N. *The mentally ill defendant in the criminal justice system.* Master's thesis, Stanford Law School, 1982.

Model Penal Code, American Law Institute, 1962.

Monahan, J. *The clinical prediction of violent behavior.* Rockville, Md.: National Institute of Mental Health, 1981.

Morse, S. J. Law and mental health professionals: The limits of expertise. *Professional Psychology,* 1978, *9,* 389–399.

Osterlind v. Hill, 263 Mass. 73, 160 N.E. 301 (1928).

Patterson, G. R. The aggressive child: Victim and architect of a coercive system. In E. J. Mash, L. A. Hamerlynck, & L. C. Handy (Eds.), *Behavior modification and families.* New York: Brunner/Mazel, 1976.

Prosser, W. L. *Handbook of the law of torts* (4th ed.). St. Paul, Minn.: West Publishing, 1971.

Restatement 2d Torts, § 314, Comment (1965).

Richards v. Stanley, 43 Cal. 2d 60, 65, 271 P. 2d 23 (1954).

Rosenhan, D. L. On being sane in insane places. *Science,* 1973, *179,* 250–258.

Rosenhan, D. L., & Seligman, M. E. P. *Abnormal psychology.* New York: Norton, in press.

Rouse v. Cameron, 373 F. 2d 451 (D.C. Cir. 1966).

Spitzer, R. L. On pseudoscience in science, logic in remission, and psychiatric diagnosis: A critique of Rosenhan's "On being sane in insane places." *Journal of Abnormal Psychology,* 1975, *84,* 442–452.

Steadman, H. J., Monahan, J., Hartstone, E., Davis, S. K., & Robbins, P. C. Mentally disordered offenders: A national survey of patients and facilities. *Law and Human Behavior,* 1982, *6,* 31–38.

Stone, A. A. The *Tarasoff* decisions: Suing psychotherapists to safeguard society. *Harvard Law Review,* 1976, *90,* 358–378.

Szasz, T. S. *The manufacture of madness.* New York: Delta, 1970.

Tarasoff v. Regents, 17 Cal. 3d at 434, 131 Cal. Rptr. at 22, citing Prosser, *supra* note 16, at 332–333 (3d ed. 1964).

Tarasoff v. Regents, 529 P. 2d 55, 118 Cal. Rptr. 129 (1974) (often called Tarasoff I).

Tarasoff v. Regents, 17 Cal. 3d 425, 431, 131 Cal. Rptr. 14, 20, 551 P. 2d 334 (1976) (often called Tarasoff II).

United States v. Freeman, 357 F. 2d 606, 622–625 (2d Cir. 1966).

Wallerstein, J. S., & Kelly, J. B. *Surviving the breakup: How children and parents cope with divorce.* New York: Basic Books, 1980.

Wexler, D. B. Patients, therapists, and third parties: The victimological virtues of Tarasoff. *International Journal of Law and Psychiatry,* 1979, *2,* 1–28.

Where the public peril begins: A survey of psychotherapists to determine the effects of *Tarasoff.* Stanford Law Review, 1978, *31,* 165.

Wigmore, J. H. Professor Münsterberg and the psychology of testimony: Being a report of the case of *Cokestone v. Münsterberg. Illinois Law Review,* 1909, *3,* 399–434.

Wootton, H. Book review of A. Goldstein, The insanity defense. *Yale Law Journal,* 1968, *77,* 1026–27.

Wyatt v. Stickney, 325 F. Supp. 781 (M.D. Ala. 1971), 344 F. Supp. 373 (M.D. Ala. 1972).

Yania v. Bigan, 397 Pa. 316, 155 A. 2d 343 (1959).

SHARI SEIDMAN DIAMOND

ORDER IN THE COURT: CONSISTENCY IN CRIMINAL-COURT DECISIONS

S hari Seidman Diamond, associate professor of psychology and criminal justice at the University of Illinois at Chicago, received her doctorate in social psychology from Northwestern University in 1972. She has held research positions at the Center for Studies in Criminal Justice of the University of Chicago Law School and in the Law Department of the London School of Economics.

Diamond's research, published in both law reviews and social science journals, has focused on legal decision making by laypersons and legal professionals and on methodological problems of research on law. Her work on the six-member jury was cited by the U.S. Supreme Court in *Ballew v. Georgia*. Because of Diamond's research on sentencing she was appointed as the psychologist member of the National Academy of Sciences Panel on Sentencing Research. She has edited a special issue of *Law and Human Behavior* on simulation research and the law and a special issue of *Law and Society Review* on psychology and law.

Diamond was a founding member of Division 41 (Psychology and Law) of the American Psychological Association. She has served on the board of directors of the American Psychology–Law Society and serves on numerous editorial boards and on the board of trustees of the Law and Society Association.

SHARI SEIDMAN DIAMOND

ORDER IN THE COURT: CONSISTENCY IN CRIMINAL-COURT DECISIONS

J ustice stands with her scales in hand: The physical weights depict a dependability of legal outcomes that should inspire confidence in the reliability of court decisions. Yet this image of the legal decision as ordered and predictable has come under considerable attack. Psychologists as well as other observers of the legal system worry, or else are convinced, that the outcomes of criminal trials are uncertain, inconsistent, and biased. A substantial portion of the research on law done by psychologists since the late 1960s can be traced to our belief in the disorder of such decision making and to our confidence that advice grounded in psychological research would improve the situation. In much of my own work I have been preoccupied with inconsistency or disparity (particularly in sentencing), its sources, and the means of reducing it.

In this paper I will argue that
- images both of order and disorder are to some extent accurate;
- the charges of disorder in part arise from misperception of the level of disorder and from unrealistic expectations about how consistent legal decisions *can* be; and
- *despite* misestimates and delusions of grandeur, some of what psychologists have learned and can learn about the decisions of criminal courts may shed light on the sources of inconsistency, identify areas in which changes can and cannot be made, and suggest ways in which order in the court can be promoted.

Inconsistency in Complex Human Judgments

The first consideration is how inconsistent criminal-court decisions actually are. *Consistency* here refers to the probability that the outcome in a given case would be the same if the case—the defendant and the offense—were cloned to produce an identical twin and that twin were sent through the system.

Consistency in the sense that the outcomes will be identical is not the only good that one might demand from a system of justice. A system might, for example, treat all accused shoplifters equally and might cut off a hand of the accused if a witness asserted that the theft had been committed. Despite consistent treatment of all those accused, we would probably conclude that such a system is unjust, that standards of proof should be more stringent, and that such a punishment is out of proportion to the offense. Yet the system of punishment would be consistent. Or we might identify a system in which cases differing in some legally irrelevant way—for example, because of the offender's sex or race—are treated differently, that is, a system with systematic bias or discrimination. If women, solely because of their sex, receive the same sentence discount from every judge, that system may be consistent—the cloned female defendant will receive the same outcome as her sister; despite this consistency and order we may find such a system unjust.

Although consistency of outcomes for identical cases may not be *enough* for a just legal system, the lack of such consistency conjures up some of the most frightening images of an unjust one. Kafka's *The Trial* (1937) is terrifying in part because of the unpredictability of the law's action; an orderly law-governed system requires that chance not be a major determinant of a case's outcome.

The Role of Chance

Popular suspicions about inconsistent legal-decision makers are captured poignantly in an old *New Yorker* magazine cartoon in which, through the closed door to the jury room, the voice is heard: "O.K., we're all in agreement . . . heads he's guilty, tails he's not." In a recent actual case a judge offered to let the flip of a coin determine a defendant's sentence.

How large a role does chance play in criminal-court decisions? We examine this question forewarned that the available data are limited; identical cases are not generally tried or sentenced more than once, and there are few satisfactory analogues to that method of assessing consistency.

Before looking at some data on the consistency of criminal-court decisions, however, I would like to consider briefly some other complex, clinical judgments that require the decision maker to evaluate and combine incomplete or potentially unreliable information to reach a decision (see Table 1). I have drawn examples from studies, representative of their respective areas, in which multiple decision makers have responded to the identical stimulus in a setting either identical to or substantially similar to their usual decision environment. The focus in these studies is on agreement between two judges. Research begun in the 1950s (e.g., Meehl, 1954; Sawyer, 1966) informed us of the relatively low validity of clinical predictions; here we concentrate not on questions of accuracy but on the less stringent goal of consistency.

Table 1
Interjudge Consistency in Complex Human Judgments

Decision makers	Stimulus	Decision	Rate of agreement between 2 judges (%)
NSF versus NAS peer reviewers[a]	150 grant proposals submitted to NSF	To fund or not to fund (half funded by NSF)	75
7 employment interviewers[b]	10 job applicants	Ranked in top 5 or in bottom 5	70
4 experienced psychiatrists[c]	153 patients interviewed twice, once by each of 2 psychiatrists	Psychosis, neurosis, character disorder	70
21–23 practicing physicians[d]	3 patient-actors with presenting symptoms (Doctors could request further information and could order and receive test results.)	Diagnosis: correct or incorrect	67, 77, 70
		Probability of agreement (both correct or both incorrect)[e]	55, 65, 57
3,576 judge–jury pairs[f]	3,576 jury trials	Guilty or not guilty	78
12 federal judges	460 presentence reports (at sentencing council)	Custody or no custody	80
8 federal judges[g]	439 presentence reports (at sentencing council)	Custody or no custody	79

[a]Cole, Cole, and Simon, 1981.
[b]Uhrbrock, 1948.
[c]Beck et al., 1962.
[d]Elstein, Shulman, and Sprafka, 1978.
[e]Inflated because physicians could also be inaccurate in different ways.
[f]Kalven and Zeisel, 1966.
[g]Diamond and Zeisel, 1975.

The first case is the recent study of National Science Foundation (NSF) peer-reviewed grant proposals. Cole, Cole, and Simon (1981) reported on a study in which 150 proposals submitted to NSF, half of which had been funded, were independently submitted to reviewers from the National Academy of Sciences (NAS). When the NSF rate of funding for these proposals was applied to the NAS ranking, the two groups agreed on 75 percent of the decisions. This rate of consistency was 50 percent better than chance, because the two would have agreed half the time even if both had responded randomly. Whether this is a respectable or distressing rate of agreement, it suggests that a rejected proposal might profitably be submitted for a second funding-decision.

The second example comes from a classic study of employment-interview decisions. Seven interviewers ranked 11 applicants following an interview (Uhrbrock, 1948). In order to compare these data with the other examples, I eliminated 1 applicant and considered that 5 of the 10 remaining applicants could be hired. The rate of agreement among all possible pairs of interviewers on who should be hired was 70 percent. Chance would have been 50 percent.

A number of studies have been conducted on psychiatric diagnosis. One well-designed example is the work of Beck, Ward, Mendelson, Mock, and Erbaugh (1962). Four experienced psychiatrists examined a series of patients. Each patient was interviewed twice, once by each of two psychiatrists. When the diagnoses were compared, Beck and his colleagues found that the diagnosticians agreed 70 percent of the time on whether the patient should be classified as psychotic, as neurotic, or as suffering from a character disorder. More recent research on psychiatric categories has achieved higher rates of agreement only in some areas. For example, 65 percent agreement was obtained by Spitzer, Forman, and Nee (1979) in field trials on the diagnosis of personality disorders.

Lest we nod our heads too quickly in recognition of the fallibility of clinical diagnosis in mental health, the next example is a study of the diagnosis of physical illness. The study, conducted by Elstein, Shulman, and Sprafka (1978), allows us to examine rates of agreement between pairs of physicians responding to three simulated cases. Each patient was an actor trained in a medical and personal history and illness. The cases were intended to be problems that a general internist could reasonably be expected to encounter in a community hospital of moderate size. Practicing physicians interviewed each patient and were provided additional data—for example, particular laboratory test results—on specific request. Most physicians reported that the simulations were convincing and provided a satisfactory approximation of the atmosphere of a real case. The results showed that an accurate diagnosis was common but hardly universal. In the first case, which required two diagnoses, two thirds of the physicians generated and continued to support both diagnoses. The second and third cases involved single diagnoses, which 77 percent and 70 percent of the physicians made correctly. If two physicians were considered to be in agreement—either they were both correct or they were both incorrect—the probability for these three cases was .55, .65, and .57.

Studies of Courtroom Consistency

In the courtroom setting, two studies bear directly on the issue of consistency. As in the grant-review and employment examples, identifying a correct diagnosis in the legal setting is difficult. Moreover, cases are rarely tried multiple times in all their complexity. What Elstein and his colleagues call high-fidelity simulations are difficult to devise in a trial context. Nearly all jury simulation studies use a single trial that is tested until the researchers are certain that the evidence is so balanced that reactions of the mock jurors will vary.[1] Two studies, however, have examined consistency in large samples of criminal trial and sentencing decisions. The first is the classic study *The American Jury* (Kalven & Zeisel, 1966), in which judges in 3,576 jury trials reported what their own verdict would have been if they, not the jury, had decided the case. On the issue of guilt—and counting hung juries as half guilty, half not-guilty—judge and jury agreed 78 percent of the time. Moreover, this rate of agreement was obtained between judge and jury for jury trials and does not indicate how frequently two *juries* would have agreed on the verdicts.

Sentencing, one might expect, creates a greater opportunity for disagreement because the decision has no factually correct solution. In fact, as I suggest later, the bases for inconsistency in sentencing mean that psychologists have more to say about inconsistency in sentencing than to say about inconsistency in guilt determination. The question of such inconsistency, or sentence disparity, was examined in a study of sentencing councils (Diamond & Zeisel, 1975). Sentencing councils exist in several federal courts. In these courts the trial judge, before pronouncing sentence, meets with other judges from the court to discuss what sentence they would favor in the particular case. Before the meeting each member of the council is given the presentence report and all other documents and facts potentially related to the sentencing decision and available to the trial judge. All participating judges, therefore, come as close to a real sentencing decision as possible, short of replacing the single trial-judge with a panel of judges.

Before a council meets, each participating judge makes and records an independent assessment of what the sentence should be, a golden opportunity to gauge the extent of disagreement among judges. Our

[1]The split is required so that variations in trial procedure (e.g., jury size) or content (e.g., nature of judicial instructions) can produce effects on verdict. That a number of simulations have failed to produce variability in their subjects' responses may be a signal of consistency.

study of two councils, one in New York and the other in Chicago, revealed a .80 probability that two judges would agree on the central question of whether to incarcerate a defendant.[2]

The methods used in the studies in Table 1 differ in various ways. Thus the agreement rate in Beck's study is reduced somewhat by the availability of a third diagnostic category, personality disorder, although this category was used much less frequently than were the two major choices, psychosis and neurosis. Although the base rate for expected agreement due to chance was approximately 50 percent for the second sentencing council, the same as in the NSF and employment interview examples, the base rate for agreement for the first council was 64 percent because of a higher rate of custody in that court.[3] The point of this table is not to suggest perfectly controlled comparisons across settings but to show that complex human judgments in both legal and nonlegal settings exhibit agreement but hardly uniform response. What distinguishes the criminal-court setting is not that its decisions are less predictable but that greater consistency is expected.

Perhaps because of the belief that criminal-court decisions are more inconsistent than they actually are or perhaps because of confidence that they could be more consistent, psychologists have studied decision making by the courts with a reformist spirit, even a messianic fervor. A closer look at the sources and controls should result in a more realistic assessment of what psychologists can contribute.

The Impact of Normal Legal Constraints on the Consistency of Criminal-Court Decisions

Two methods are used to achieve consistency in all types of court decisions. First, all legal decision-making tasks are structured by a legislatively and judicially formed framework of law. This framework not only affects what cases and evidence may be presented to the judge or jury but also sets standards and procedures for whoever will decide the case. When the decision maker is a jury, the framework provides further legal direction through instructions from the judge. Second, the legal system provides an elaborate set of after-the-fact controls—the opportunity to appeal a verdict or other decision to a higher court, which may endorse or set aside the lower court's action. In rendering a decision, an appellate court generally issues an opinion that outlines its justification for endorsing or rejecting the decision of the lower court. This decision

[2]The average rate of incarceration for cases in the Chicago sample was 57 percent; in New York the average rate was 77 percent.
[3]The chance level of agreement between two judges in Chicago was $(.57)(.57) + (.43)(.43) = .50$; in New York it was $(.77)(.77) + (.23)(.23) = .64$.

plus opinion serves as both a corrective device for the case that it directly affects and a mechanism to structure future trial decisions.

The value of appellate review was not lost on psychologist Richard Atkinson (1981), former NSF director, when he responded to the NSF peer-review study cited earlier. He noted that procedures for review had been improved since the study and cited in particular the formal appeal process now available for reconsideration of declined proposals.

If, despite the control of law and appellate review, the legal system falls short of achieving uniformly consistent decisions, the next question becomes, Why does it fall short? Discussion here focuses on criminal-court decisions, although some of it applies to civil decisions as well. I consider first some limits on the control of verdict inconsistency and then look at the effect of these and some other factors on the control of sentence inconsistency.

Verdicts

One source that limits the ability of appellate review to control inconsistency in verdicts is the nature of evidence leading to criminal-court decisions. Verdicts frequently hinge on the credibility of witnesses; the defendant denies being present when the offense was committed or disputes the prosecutor's claim about the defendant's presumed intent. Appellate courts are hesitant to overturn the verdict of someone present at the trial in favor of an impression from a paper record. The courts are willing to accept that the trial judge or jury, watching and listening to the defendant and the witnesses, could have been properly convinced of the defendant's guilt. Moreover, appellate courts are required by law to uphold a lower court's verdict if the record could have sustained it. Thus, conservativism in review is formally endorsed by the system.

A related characteristic of criminal trial-court decisions, which reduces the potential impact of appellate review, is that verdicts are delivered by judges and juries without explanation. The secretive nature of the jury verdict has troubled researchers interested in jury behavior; the secrecy also increases the likelihood that a questionable verdict will be given the benefit of the doubt and will be endorsed by an appellate court although the verdict resulted from an error or a misunderstanding by the jury. Trial court judges in bench trials, too, generally make few comments on their own verdicts. This approach reduces the likelihood that the appellate court's evaluation of the judge's verdict will be negatively colored by its disagreement with the judge's reasons. It thereby reduces the probability that the appellate court will reverse the decision, an outcome that most trial court judges are eager to avoid.

A third restraint on appellate review of verdicts results from an intentional bias in the system. Although in civil cases both the plaintiff and the defendant can appeal the verdict, in criminal cases only the defendant has the right to appeal and an acquittal is final. As a result, if chance produces an acquittal in a case that generally would have resulted in a conviction, the appellate court will not be called on to adjust the outcome. The resulting inconsistency is tolerated as part of conservativism regarding unwarranted convictions.

A fourth, and perhaps the most important, limit on the ability of the appellate court to promote consistency in criminal-court verdicts is the pervasive method of case disposal known as plea bargaining. In most jurisdictions 80 percent to 90 percent of all sentenced offenders have pleaded guilty, primarily in return for an explicit agreement with the prosecutor that a particular sentence would be recommended to the judge or that some charges would be reduced or dropped. If, as a number of researchers have suggested (e.g., Finkelstein, 1975), some innocent defendants may plead guilty in order to avoid the risk of a more serious sentence should they press their innocence and be convicted at trial, the disposition of these cases may depend primarily on the particular prosecutor's threats and offers. To the extent that prosecutors differ, inconsistent verdicts may result. Moreover, appeals are likely to be treated differently when guilty verdicts derive from pleas as opposed to trials. The defendant who has pleaded guilty is generally less able to argue convincingly that the guilty verdict was in error (*Parker v. North Carolina*, 1970).

Sentencing

If the nature of the evidence, lack of articulated reasons, one-sided appeals, and plea bargaining mitigate the effect of legal measures to increase verdict consistency, how do these features affect sentencing consistency? The first difference to note between the verdict and sentence is that the two methods—legal guidance and the right to appeal after the decision—are substantially curtailed for sentencing. Until recently, most legislative codes gave remarkably little guidance to the sentencer. For instance, the sentencer might legally sentence an offender convicted of bank robbery with force to anything from probation to 20 years in prison (18 U.S.C. § 2113[1]). Such a situation led Judge Marvin Frankel to characterize sentencing as "law without order" (Frankel, 1973). Moreover, as long as the sentencer is not sufficiently aberrant or flagrant to announce that a year is added because the offender is black or has a beard, most jurisdictions provide no right to a separate appeal on the sentence.

It is not immediately clear why U.S. law has been so hesitant to constrain sentencing decisions through legislative guidance and appellate review.[4] One possible explanation is the ambiguity of plea bargain-

[4]England has an active appellate calendar for sentence review (Thomas, 1979).

ing; offenders pleading guilty have been viewed as endorsing their sentences and therefore as not entitled to complain. That explanation does not seem entirely satisfactory. Zeisel and I (1977) examined sentence review in Connecticut and Massachusetts, two states that do provide offenders sentenced to prison with the right to appeal, albeit to a division of trial-court judges rather than to an appellate court. We found that in Connecticut sentences resulting from a conviction at trial were somewhat more likely to be modified than sentences following a plea, but that in Massachusetts trial convictions had no such edge. Thus the notion that a plea bargain psychologically reduces the argument in favor of sentence review received only partial support.

There is a second explanation for the law's hesitancy. Until recently, most states used an indeterminate sentencing structure. The judge decided whether to incarcerate, but the length of an offender's prison term was not actually determined at the time of sentencing. Later review by an administrative agency—the parole board—set the release date. The underlying rationale for this approach was a medical model in which the sentence was to be an individualized treatment, administered until a cure was effected; deciding in advance the necessary duration of the cure was presumed impossible. Thus lack of attention to consistency in sentencing could be justified because the term announced by the judge did not accurately predict the actual sentence length. One weakness in this explanation is that even under completely indeterminate sentencing schemes the judge still had to make the most crucial decision: whether or not to incarcerate.

The current movement to reform sentencing has attempted to rectify the lack of judicial guidance and minimal appellate review. Responding to complaints about sentence inconsistency or sentence disparity, and attempting to avoid mandatory sentences that would eliminate judicial discretion, judges in some states have produced or have worked with researchers to produce sentencing guidelines. In most versions these guidelines indicate a range of sentences that will normally be considered appropriate for a particular offense and offender combination, so that the sentencing judge can check the guideline to learn the lowest and highest sentences that most offenders convicted of a third burglary might expect. Because most guideline systems have been entirely voluntary, however,[5] and allow relatively wide ranges of sentences within the guideline, studies have detected few, if any, effects of the guidelines on sentencing (Rich, Sutton, Clear, & Saks, 1981).

It is tempting to conclude that judicial resistance to constraints on sentencing decisions stems from an unreasoned objection to external directives. Judges live with such constraints in other areas of their decision making, however; thus looking further into the construction of sen-

[5]Minnesota is an important exception. When a judge does not use the Minnesota guideline sentence, the judge must give reasons for deviating. Both guideline and nonguideline sentences are reviewable by the appellate court.

tence disparity for other explanations is worthwhile. A psychological analysis of the sentencing decision offers some insights. I will return to this topic as I discuss areas in which psychological research has provided or can provide theory and research on sources of and remedies for inconsistency in criminal-court decisions.

Psychological Research on Inconsistency in Criminal-Court Decisions

This discussion of psychological research on the consistency of criminal-court decisions covers three topics. The first topic, the identity of the decision maker, has already received substantial attention from psychologists in research primarily on jury size; the impact of that research has been felt in major Supreme Court decisions. The second topic, sources of sentence inconsistency, has received some attention from psychologists, but there is a good deal more to do. I suggest some directions that research might take. Finally, I discuss some procedural variations in selection, instruction, and formulation of decision requirements for the jury. Little about this last topic is known, but interesting lines of research are being or could be pursued.

Identity of the Decision Maker

Much research by psychologists interested in law in the past decade has focused on the composition of the jury. If all potential jurors exposed to the same trial reacted with the same verdict, jury composition would have no implications for verdict consistency. The best estimate, however, is that the jury's first ballot is unanimous only 30 percent of the time (Kalven & Zeisel, 1966). Variables that affect the initial vote distribution and influence transformation of initial disagreement into a verdict can be crucial for understanding verdict consistency.

Jury size. In 1970 the Supreme Court ruled in *Williams v. Florida* that state juries as small as six persons were constitutionally permissible in criminal cases. Had the Court found justification for permitting the reduction in jury size only by concluding that the Constitution did not guarantee a jury of twelve, or had the Court relied solely on historical arguments that the framers of the Constitution had purposefully left jury size unspecified, psychologists and other social scientists would have had little to offer. Instead, the Supreme Court justified its decision on behavioral grounds, namely, that a reduction in size from 12 to 6 would have no effect on jury decisions. In drawing this conclusion, the Court relied on scanty evidence (some casual observations and unsupported assertions), and researchers responded to the Court's decision with criticism about its logic (Zeisel, 1971) and with empirical work that attempted to test the hypothesis of no difference due to jury size.

The next Court test for jury size occurred in 1973; in *Colgrove v. Battin* the Supreme Court extended its endorsement of juries as small as six to federal civil trials. This time the conclusion that jury size has no effect on verdict was bolstered by what the Court called "convincing empirical evidence." Examination revealed that the evidence consisted of four seriously flawed studies (Zeisel & Diamond, 1974). Between 1974 and 1978 a number of more carefully designed studies appeared (e.g., Saks, 1977). When the Court decided in *Ballew v. Georgia* that juries as small as five could not be depended on to render reliable verdicts, the majority opinion cited the available theory and new research pointing to a difference between six-person and twelve-person juries. No research was reported on differences between five-person and six-person juries; probably none existed. Though the evidence used to bolster the majority opinion in *Ballew* logically warranted a reversal of the two earlier decisions on six-person juries, the Court did not reverse itself and did not require twelve-member juries. (One of the ways, however, in which the Supreme Court avoids some inconsistency is that it is rarely willing to consider the same specific issue twice in so small a space of time.)

Some questions about jury size have centered on the jury's ability as a fact finder and on the consequences of better fact finding for more accurate verdicts. The question of concern here is, would the verdicts of twelve-person juries in the same case be more consistent than the verdicts of the same number of six-person juries? Sampling theory predicts greater consistency for the twelve-member jury, because the probability of six unusual persons on a jury is far greater than that of twelve unusual persons. Jurors' verdicts, however, do not emerge from a statistical combination of independent juror preferences; thus questions about group process are important. If, for example, a larger jury were to inhibit the participation of most jurors, verdicts might be determined by the inclination of only two or three of the most aggressive members on a twelve-person jury. If a smaller jury did not have the same inhibiting effect, the effective pool of decision makers on a six-member jury might actually be larger than that on a larger jury, and the sampling predictions for effects of jury size would not be accurate.

The empirical studies testing the effects of jury size support the predictions based on sampling theory, despite more equal verbal production by members of six-person juries. The position of the majority on the first ballot is the one generally adopted by the jury. Sampling logic holds here too: The majority position of two twelve-person juries responding to the same trial is more likely to be the same than the majority position of two six-person juries responding to the same trial, with all jurors drawn from the same population.

A large (12-member) jury is thus a safeguard that can protect the consistency of jury verdicts. This protective role is recognized even in states often using smaller juries—a jury of 12 is preserved in capital cases. Significantly the value of decision-making groups is also recognized in other parts of the legal system. Appellate courts generally have three or more judges, so that a reversal by an appellate court does not simply substitute the judgment of one judge for another. Moreover, the size of the appellate court increases with the importance and finality of its decision. For example, Illinois Appellate Court decisions are rendered by three judges, but Illinois Supreme Court cases go before a tribunal of seven (Constitution of Illinois, 1970, 6:3,5). The U.S. Supreme Court, of course, consists of nine members.

Single judge versus lay panel. A controversial issue in the courts and among scholars is whether there are civil cases so complex that the Fifth Amendment right to due process is violated by a jury's deciding the case. Richard Lempert (1981) has identified the key question as whether a judge sitting in lieu of a jury can do better.[6] He suggests that research may identify the jury as a "minimax" solution "not as efficient or as rational as trial to the better judges, but never sinking to the levels of inefficiency, irrationality, or bias that characterize the worst of the bench" (p. 95). This analysis highlights another dimension that may affect consistency when legal training is accompanied by strong opinions: The price of potential expertise in the single decision maker may also purchase extreme or idiosyncratic views.

A partial test of this trade-off has emerged in a study that I have been conducting in the English magistrates' courts in London under a grant from the Law and Social Sciences Program of the National Science Foundation. The major purpose of the study is to compare the decision making by the lay and professional magistrates in criminal cases. The lay magistrates and the legally trained professionals have the same general jurisdiction: They set bail in all criminal cases brought to court; they decide on guilt and sentence the offenders in 98 percent of all criminal cases. Only a few crimes, like murder and rape, must be sent to the higher Crown Court for trial before a jury. All cases tried in the Crown Court must be decided by a jury of 12; bench trials do not occur. The defendant in the magistrates' court, which sees the bulk of criminal work, may appear before a single legally qualified professional magistrate, called a *stipendiary,* or before a panel of lay magistrates. The panel of lay magistrates is the dominant form of tribunal; but, in the big cities where the caseload is heavy, stipendiaries share the work. This research was conducted in three London courts where three or four stipendiaries sit in separate courtrooms down the hall from rotating panels of lay magistrates.

A variety of data was collected on this project. Cases were observed and coded in three courts where 10 stipendiaries and a large number of

[6]This important point is missed in much of the psychological research on jury behavior. The jury is generally compared to an abstract standard of perfect recall or impartiality rather than to the alternative human institution it replaces, the judge.

lay justices sat. The magistrates' questions were recorded as fully as possible—there are no court reporters in these courts and taping was not permitted—along with case characteristics, defendant behavior, and decisions. Nearly 400 hours of hearings were coded. In order to trace progress and outcome on a series of more homogeneous cases, we drew separate samples of theft and burglary cases from the files of the three courts. Finally, I interviewed nearly half the London stipendiaries and 36 lay magistrates. During the interviews the magistrates were asked to make sentence recommendations in response to several case descriptions.

Across all three simulation cases in which custody was a conceivable choice, in the burglary and theft file samples, and in the field observations, stipendiaries were more likely to recommend or actually give custody sentences. This sentencing pattern suggests that legal training, more extensive court experience, or some other individual difference leads the professionals to be more severe in their sentencing. A closer look at the data, however, indicates that this explanation is incomplete. The interview data compare individual responses; there the professionals are simply more severe. The field data compare panels of lay magistrates with professionals who sit singly. Those data show that stipendiaries are both more likely to give custody sentences *and* are more likely to give the least severe sentence, a conditional discharge; the lay panels are more moderate. The group decision appeared to moderate the sentences of the individual lay judges, while the single magistrate, who did not need to justify a chosen sentence to colleagues, was free to take an extreme position without fear of contradiction. Thus, the heaven-inspired sentence of the unusually wise professional may be sacrificed before the lay panel, but so will the sentence that receives its inspiration from a not-so-heavenly source.[7]

Sources of Sentence Disparity

If pairs of judges disagree in one of five cases on whether an offender should be incarcerated, and their rate of disagreement climbs if disagreements on length of sentence are also considered, how does this disagreement come about? One common explanation is that judges are basically tough or lenient and these differences in overall severity level produce sentences that vary with the judge's identity. A number of stud-

[7]The group polarization phenomenon (Lamm & Myers, 1978) might appear to contradict this conclusion, for it suggests that a group decision will be more extreme than the average of its individual member preferences. There are, however, two explanations why group polarization is not inconsistent with those results. First, the group decision may still be less extreme than its most extreme member's individual preference. Second, group polarization serves to accentuate an initial group preference, but, as Stephenson and Brotherton (1975) have shown, polarization does not occur when individuals differ initially in the direction of their preference.

ies have compared overall rates of particular sentences given by different judges and have shown that some judges give custody sentences more frequently than other judges (e.g., Gaudet, Harris, & John, 1933; Thomsen, 1962). One difficulty with using these data to draw conclusions about differences between judges is the assumption that judges are responding to equivalent sets of cases. Moreover, because aggregate sentence levels are compared, we cannot tell whether judges simply differ in the threshold that they use to produce custody or are incarcerating different types of offenders.

The study of sentencing councils provided data on a large sample of sentencing opportunities along with the preferred sentence of a number of judges for each case. By looking at the responses of this set of judges it was possible to test whether the sentences preferred by Judge X were regularly more severe than those preferred by the others (Diamond, 1981). Although the data revealed that judges did differ in their average sentence levels—so that some were on the average likely to propose a more severe sentence than their colleagues on the same case—there was considerable overlap: Judges who were most severe on some cases were least severe on others.

In searching for other clues on the sources of disparity, I looked at the cases themselves. Cases that evoked disagreement over custody were not a random subset of cases. Two significant kinds of cases produced conflict among the judges. First were those with both mitigating and aggravating factors. Thus, Judge X could choose a sentence of probation for a first offender who committed a serious offense by focusing on the mitigation of youth and no prior record; Judge Y, emphasizing the magnitude of the current offense, might advocate a custodial sentence. The second type of case that stimulated disagreement over custody featured a single characteristic that suggested both high culpability and a good prognosis. The offender with stable personal relationships or an education has less excuse for illegal behavior but may also be viewed as less likely to recidivate. The classic example is the tax evader or embezzler, an apparent pillar of the community before indictment on the present charge. Should the person be treated as an example so that others will be discouraged from crime by such treatment, or, in acknowledging the low probability that the offender will sin again, should the defendant be placed on probation, fined, or made to do community service?

Disagreement on goals. The various possible responses by judges and other court observers to this kind of question may partially explain why clear legal guidance in sentencing is lacking in both legislation and appellate review. Decision makers generally share the same goal for a verdict—accuracy—and disagree only on how that is to be achieved. There is no such necessary agreement among decision makers on the purposes of a particular sentence. When talking last year to an English magistrate, I was confronted with the inherent difficulty in evaluating a sentencing strategy. He reported that when an umbrella peddler without

CRIMINAL-COURT DECISIONS

a license appeared in his courtroom, the magistrate always asked if it had been raining when the fellow was arrested. The magistrate was pleased to discover that a colleague asked the same question. The difficulty arose with the answer. The magistrate whom I was interviewing explained that he increased the fine if it had been raining because business was good, but he reported that the colleague's analysis brought a different decision. If it had been raining the colleague *reduced* the penalty because the umbrella salesman had been providing a service. The serious lesson of this story is that, in at least some situations, different sentencing purposes appear to suggest entirely different sentence outcomes.

Examining the two major types of sentencing goals—retribution and crime reduction—helps to organize some of the patterns of disagreement observed in the sentencing council data. The retributivist position on sentencing stresses the primary goal of a sentence as payment by the offender for the offense. The focus on the offender's past rather than future behavior can be seen in the position of the classical retributivist, Kant, who argued that members of an isolated island society deciding to disband and disperse would have to execute all imprisoned murderers or "be regarded as accomplices in the public violation of legal justice" (trans., 1965). In contrast the focus of the utilitarian position is crime reduction (Cross, 1975). Sentences that stress this goal adopt a forward-looking stance: What sentence will reduce the likelihood that the offender or others who learn of the sentence will commit additional offenses? (Hart, 1968). While sentencers may wish to achieve both goals, if they differ in which goal they emphasize, will they favor different sentences? A study by Hogarth (1971) suggests that they will. Hogarth conducted research on the attitudes and sentencing behavior of Ontario magistrates and classified the magistrates on their sentencing patterns. His analysis indicates that an emphasis on different sentencing goals can explain some between-judge inconsistencies in sentences. This was one of the findings that led to the title of his book, *Sentencing as a Human Process.*

Although Hogarth's data show a correlation between goals and sentence choice, his data do not tell us whether the goal produces the sentence or merely justifies a sentence chosen for other reasons. A study by McFatter (1978) suggests the influence of sentencing goals on sentence choice. McFatter instructed a group of subjects to sentence in accordance with a retributive philosophy. Their recommended sentences differed systematically from the sentences recommended by those instructed to use utilitarian sentencing goals.

To the extent that basic and unresolved disagreements about moral philosophy underlie some of the inconsistencies in sentencing behavior, the courts' reluctance to provide clear guidance in this area may not be surprising. If such philosophical differences offered the primary explanation for sentence inconsistency, the role of the psychologist in reducing inconsistency would be simply to provide data on the pattern of disagreement in sentencing goals and the effect of these goals on preferred punishments so that legislative bodies or sentencing commissions would be informed of public or judicial opinions on the subject. But psychological theory and empirical research on sentencing may make a more substantial contribution. Goals are not adopted in a vacuum. Although Hogarth's (1971) work suggests that judges generally favor certain goals across cases, sentencing goals appear to depend also on the particular type of case. Thus more than half of the English magistrates in my study, in response to a case of shoplifting, reported that their goal in sentencing was to change the offender's behavior, but only one fourth aimed the sentence at changing the activities of a burglar with previous convictions. More magistrates in the second case were concerned with retribution and a lesson for the general public. These results indicate that although goals may differ across judges, a judge's goals also vary according to the type of case. One judge who tends to favor rehabilitation may adopt a just deserts posture for drug offenders, whereas another who generally maintains a just deserts orientation may focus primarily on rehabilitation when a sex offense is involved. A full explanation of sentencing must explain these within-judge discriminations as well as between-judge differences.

Sentencing goals and attributions. Psychologists have recently spent a good deal of time investigating attributions of causality (e.g., Heider, 1958; Weiner, 1974). Attribution theory offers a promising set of concepts for the investigation of sentencing behavior. The model in Figure 1 attempts to show linkages between sentencing goals and attributions. The three stages indicate general goals that a sentencer may hold: individual crime reduction, the deterrence of others, and retribution. Although a sentencer may have all three goals, some choices or differences in emphasis will occur. One potential determinant of the choice is a moral stance. For example, general deterrence may be rejected if the sentencer feels that it is morally impermissible to punish someone for the effect that the punishment will have on others. The choice of a general goal may also be affected by attributions of causality either for crime as a whole or by particular offense-offender combinations. Thus a retributionist who believes that society is entitled or even obligated to punish an offender in proportion to the violation makes the attribution that the individual chooses to violate the law even though free not to violate it.

The three stages in the model are ordered to illustrate more clearly that the retributive goal can also be adopted by default; the sentencer may reject individual crime reduction and general deterrence strategies not because they are morally unacceptable[8] but because the sentencer is convinced either that they do not work generally or that they cannot

[8]The strict retributionist rejects instrumental purposes of sentencing on the grounds that people should be punished for what they have done, not for the potential impact of their sentence on their or others' future behavior.

Stage 1. Individual crime reduction as a goal? (If not, go to Stage 2.)

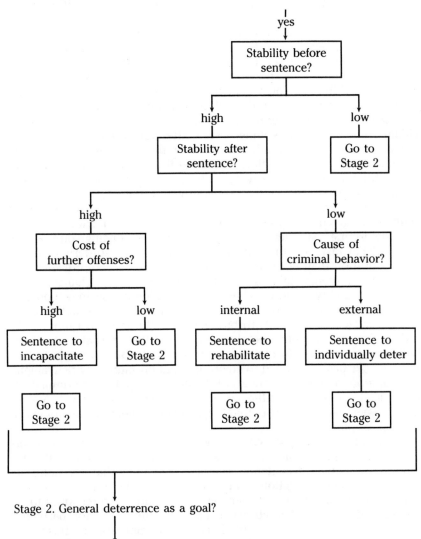

Figure 1. Sentencing goals and attributions

work for this kind of offender or offense. The dominant philosophy of sentencing in the United States for many years has been to reform the offender. Recently emphasis has shifted to a just deserts, or retributive, model (e.g., von Hirsch, 1976; Fogel, 1975). At least one explanation for the shift has been that the cumulative impact of evidence that rehabilitation has not affected recidivism has led to skepticism about reform as a realistic sentencing goal (e.g., Lipton, Martinson, & Wilks, 1975; Brody, 1976).

The model suggests that willingness to consider a general crime-reduction goal requires further attributions by the sentencer about the stability and internality of the causes of the offender's crime behavior. The first attribution question is how stable the behavior will be without a sentence. If the sentencer concludes that the behavior was what the English magistrates call a one-off thing—highly unlikely to recur whatever sentence the offender receives—then further consideration of individual crime reduction is unnecessary; attention shifts directly to general deterrence and retribution. If, however, the behavior is judged to be stable, the sentencer must decide whether it will have a high probability of repetition in response to every sentence or whether an available sentencing choice can reduce the probability of further offenses. If the stability of the behavior is considered irrevocably high no matter what sentence is given, a decision about the cost of the behavior to society will determine whether an incapacitation sentencing purpose is adopted. For instance, the annoyance of drunk and disorderly behavior or prostitution may not warrant a substantial intervention even when the behavior seems stable and resistant to attempts to change.

If the stability of criminal behavior is considered low in response to possible sentences, a further attribution involves the internality of the crime's causes. An internal attribution directs the sentencer to rehabilitation. The offender must be changed so that the internal roots of the behavior are altered. In contrast an external attribution suggests that the offender has responded to environmental pressures; by rearranging the reinforcement contingencies of the behavior, potential criminal activity can be altered. Thus the shoplifter is given a heavy fine or a night in jail to persuade him or her that the benefits of offending are not worth the risk of punishment.

Thus, empirical research has shown that judges emphasize different sentencing goals and that the selection of a sentencing goal is related to the choice of sentence. The next step—one that psychologists are in an excellent position to take (Diamond & Herhold, 1981)—is to explore the connections between causal attributions in response to offender and offense characteristics and the preference for particular goals.[9] The model I have presented may offer a framework for this investigation. In the process of studying the foundations of sentencing prefer-

[9]Although judges have been identified as the sentencers in this discussion, there is substantial evidence that prosecutors and probation officers (e.g., Ebbesen & Konečni, 1981) may have a major influence on sentencing outcomes. The research agenda outlined in this section therefore is meant to be applied to these decision makers as well. Some research by John Carroll on parole board members (Carroll, 1978; Carroll & Payne, 1977) has already been conducted; attributions of stability have emerged as significant predictors of parole release decisions.

ence, psychologists may illuminate some of the sources of disparity across decision makers and lay the groundwork for increased consistency in sentencing.

Some Procedural Factors in Jury Trials With Uncertain Effects on Consistency

Do the procedures for selecting the members of a jury affect the consistency of jury verdicts? There is much debate about this (e.g., Kairys, Schulman, & Harring, 1975; Saks, 1976; Bermant, 1975). Attorneys often claim that they occasionally win their cases during the voir dire, or jury selection. In the early 1970s psychologists and other social scientists began to help attorneys select juries in a number of highly publicized cases (Schulman, Shaver, Colman, Enrich, & Christie, 1973) with so-called scientific jury selection. In this method a community survey of potential jurors is conducted to identify characteristics associated with friendly or unfriendly attitudes toward the parties in the case. These patterns are then used during jury selection to identify and excuse potential jurors unlikely to be sympathetic to the client. Thus, a survey might reveal that male community members who read the *New York Times* and own their own business are, compared to other groups, less sympathetic with a self-defense argument for acquittal. If the attorney plans that defense for the client, the survey will warn the attorney to excuse such jurors. In a case that has had substantial pretrial publicity, the survey may ask how respondents feel about the probable guilt or innocence of the specific defendant in the case and then relate this opinion to other juror characteristics that will be used to select the jury.

A number of observers (e.g., Etzioni, 1974) have expressed alarm at this activity, concerned that these techniques may create an unfair advantage for the party with resources to invest in such assistance. The evidence does not indicate cause for concern. Though there is some evidence that attorneys do somewhat better than chance at identifying and removing unfriendly jurors (Zeisel & Diamond, 1978), it is unclear whether the addition of social science survey data increases the attorney's effectiveness in this regard. Laboratory efforts to predict individual juror responses in simulated trials have consistently been unable to explain much variation in verdict preferences based on juror attitudes and background characteristics (for a review, see Saks & Hastie, 1978). I suspect that the successful attorney selection efforts in our study of voir dire were due more to the clear signals given by some jurors than to the unusual insight of a few attorneys. But we need to know more about the effects of jury selection than the available data can tell us before we conclude that it is either valuable or disruptive. The best advice for a lawyer is still to spend time in preparing the evidence rather than in pouring over a printout from a juror survey. Thorough legal representation is also likely to be the strategy best suited to promoting verdict consistency.

Instability in jury verdicts can also be produced if jurors do not understand the law they are meant to apply. The legal instruction to the jury is a procedural control that has recently received substantial research attention from a number of psychologists. Work by Elwork, Sales, and Alfini (1982) and others (Charrow & Charrow, 1979; Severance & Loftus, 1982) has shown the weakness of typical jury instructions. As read by the judge from an approved list so that they are guaranteed to be legally correct, such instructions generally are unevenly comprehended by the jurors whom they are meant to instruct. The work of all these researchers in rewriting instructions for improved comprehensibility has been quite successful.

But there is another step. Juries are typically instructed on the law only *after* they have heard all the evidence in the case. Recalling information is easier when it makes sense—de Groot's 1965 study of chess players showed that skilled players were able to remember chess positions better than amateurs only when the chess pieces were arranged in real board positions; the experts showed no memory advantage when the pieces were arranged randomly. By instructing the jurors *before* they hear the evidence on items like the elements of the offense that must be proved before a conviction may be returned, the law can provide a structure to focus the jurors' attention on critical data. Because of the danger that early instruction may promote premature conclusions before all the evidence is presented, exploring the effects of adding early legal instruction on jury retention of information and decision making would be useful.

Finally, a third procedural variable that may affect verdict consistency is the structure of the decision task. In complex legal decision tasks, items of evidence must be individually evaluated and the evaluations must then be combined to reach a global conclusion like guilty or not guilty. Psychologists studying judgment have shown that judges are substantially less internally consistent when asked mentally to combine reactions to such evidence than when they are asked to evaluate individual items of evidence (Schum & Martin, 1982). Jurors are instructed on the elements of an offense and the separate judgments about action and intent that are required for a conviction, but they are generally left to their own devices to consider these separate judgments or not in arriving at a verdict. Although leaving the aggregate decision of the jury untouched may be desirable (leaving room, for example, for jury nullification), the jury can be specifically instructed to decide on each element separately before considering what the overall verdict ought to be.

Empirical work is needed here, too, to examine whether the verdicts of juries who receive such direction in structuring their decision making are more consistent with one another than those of juries whose decisions are not structured in this manner. Similar questions can be raised about other procedural variations (e.g., method for selection of a jury foreman, instruction on the timing of vote taking in the juryroom, use of secret or open ballots). Although I have been among those psychologists who have complained that psychologists interested in law should broaden their horizons beyond the jury box, in the search for consistency there may still be much to learn from the jury.

Conclusion

What do these observations indicate about the prospects for consistency in criminal-court decisions and for the ability of psychological research to promote it? First, comparisons with nonlegal tasks show that such legal decisions are not uniquely inconsistent, nor do they appear to be substantially less consistent than other complex human judgments. Yet an element of chance appears to influence verdict and sentence outcomes. Given the opportunity, most observers would prefer to see the role of chance reduced.

Second, when traditional legal efforts to promote consistency through structure and review were examined, a number of obstacles that reduce the impact of these efforts were identified. Some obstacles, like the reluctance to review verdicts of acquittal, reflect values that supersede the goal of consistency. Thus there may be natural and enduring limits to the success of consistency-promoting activities.

These explorations should stimulate a more sober appraisal of the scope of potentially reducible inconsistency. In the desire to reform, psychologists interested in law have too frequently overdramatized legal weakness and have shown unbridled optimism about the strength of social variables and psychological intervention. Courtroom decisions are not as unreliable as feared, and reforms are not as powerful as their designers desire.

As a result of our misperceptions, we psychologists have often failed or appeared to fail in our attempt to identify meaningful differences: We have designed research capable of hitting only unrealistically large targets, and we have evaluated differences against standards of potential impact that might gently be characterized as delusions of grandeur. Our expedition to capture the effects of jury size would have proceeded more swiftly had investigators recognized early in their search that the target was a small, albeit nutritious, fish and not the great white whale. Instead, many researchers conducted studies predictably too low in power to detect the small effects that should have been anticipated.

Realistically I should not have been surprised or disappointed that the group process effects of the sentencing councils reduced disparity

143

by a modest 10 percent. The legal system has numerous checks and balances; it is a homeostatic organism in which interventions in one part are rapidly compensated for by adjustments elsewhere. Interventions at a single point are likely to have only limited impact. Full-scale attacks on inconsistency require a larger view.

My discussion also suggests that research on inconsistency might profitably be supplemented by an investigation of the sources of inconsistency, which may be as illuminating as our attempts to control it. The regularity of judicial disagreement in sentencing can shed light on conflicts between sentencing goals that must be resolved normatively before sentencing consistency can be substantially increased. The apparent inability of jurors to understand particular instructions may signal not only juror ignorance and a lack of instruction clarity but also trouble spots in the legal concepts themselves. Jurors' uneven interpretation of the conspiracy instruction, for example, may highlight basic difficulties in the conspiracy law and not simply in the way the law is communicated.

The relation between psychology and law has been recognized for many years (e.g., Munsterberg, 1915), but the enormous growth and gradual maturation of research in this area has only a recent history (Diamond, 1982; Monahan & Loftus, 1982). We have explored how psychological research has been applied to questions of consistency in trial-court decisions. Potential contributions by psychological research to an understanding of legal decision making are even greater. If realistic goals and research strategies are adopted, we may even find our results promoting greater order in the court.

References

Atkinson, R. C. The peer review question. Letter to the editor. *Science*, 1981, *214*, 1292.

Ballew v. Georgia, 435 U.S. 223 (1978).

Beck, A. T., Ward, C. H., Mendelson, M., Mock, J. E., & Erbaugh, J. K. Reliability of psychiatric diagnoses: A study of consistency of clinical judgments and ratings. *American Journal of Psychiatry*, 1962, *119*, 351–357.

Bermant, G. The notion of conspiracy is not tasty to Americans. *Psychology Today*, 1975, *8*, 60–67.

Brody, S. R. *The effectiveness of sentencing—A review of the literature.* London: Her Majesty's Stationery Office, 1976.

Carroll, J. S. Causal attributions in expert parole decisions. *Journal of Personality and Social Psychology*, 1978, *36*, 1501–1511.

Carroll, J. S., & Payne, J. W. Crime seriousness, recidivism risk, and causal attributions in judgments of prison term by students and experts. In B. D. Sales (Ed.), *Perspectives in law and psychology: Vol. I. Criminal justice system.* New York: Plenum, 1977, pp. 191–240.

Charrow, R. P., & Charrow, V. R. Making legal language understandable: A psycholinguistic study of jury instructions. *Columbia Law Review*, 1979, *79*, 1306–74.

Cole, S., Cole, J. R., & Simon, G. A. Chance and consensus in peer review. *Science*, 1981, *214*, 881–886.

Colgrove v. Battin, 413 U.S. 149 (1973).

Constitution of Illinois, 1970.

Cross, Sir Rupert. *The English sentencing system* (2nd ed.). London: Butterworths, 1975.

de Groot, A. D. Het denken van den Schaker [Thought and choice in chess]. The Hague: Mouton, 1965.

Diamond, S. S. Exploring patterns in sentence disparity. In B. D. Sales (Ed.), *Perspectives in law and psychology: Vol. II. The trial process.* New York: Plenum, 1981.

Diamond, S. S. Growth and maturation in psychology and law. *Law and Society Review,* 1982, *17,* 11–20.

Diamond, S. S., & Herhold, C. J. Understanding criminal sentencing: Views from law and social psychology. In G. M. Stephenson & J. H. Davis (Eds.), *Progress in applied social psychology.* Chichester: Wiley, 1981.

Diamond, S. S., & Zeisel, H. Sentencing councils: A study of sentence disparity and its reduction. *University of Chicago Law Review,* 1975, *43,* 109–149.

Ebbesen, E., & Konečni, V. The processing of sentencing adult felons. In B. D. Sales (Ed.), *The trial process.* New York: Plenum, 1981.

Elstein, A. S., Schulman, L. S., & Sprafka, S. A. *Medical problem solving: An analysis of clinical reasoning.* Cambridge: Harvard University Press, 1978.

Elwork, A., Sales, B. D., & Alfini, J. *Writing understandable jury instructions.* Charlottesville, Va.: Michie/Bobbs-Merrill, 1982.

Etzioni, A. Creating an imbalance. *Trial,* 1974, *10,* 28ff.

Finkelstein, M. O. A statistical analysis of guilty plea practices in Federal Courts. *Harvard Law Review,* 1975, *89,* 293.

Fogel, D. *We are the living proof. The justice model for corrections.* Cincinnati: Anderson, 1975.

Frankel, M. *Criminal sentences: Law without order.* New York: Hill and Wang, 1973.

Gaudet, F. J., Harris, G. S., & St. John, C. W. Individual differences in the sentencing tendencies of judges. *Journal of Criminal Law, Criminology, and Police Science,* 1933, *23,* 811–816.

Hart, H. L. A. *Punishment and responsibility.* Oxford: Oxford University Press, 1968.

Heider, F. The psychology of interpersonal relations. New York: Wiley, 1958.

Hogarth, J. *Sentencing as a human process.* Toronto: University of Toronto Press, 1971.

Kafka, F. *The trial.* New York: Alfred A. Knopf, 1937.

Kairys, D., Schulman, J., & Harring, S. (Eds.). *The jury system: New methods for reducing prejudice.* Philadelphia: National Lawyers Guild, 1975.

Kalven, H., Jr., & Zeisel, H. *The American jury.* Boston: Little, Brown, 1966.

Kant, I. [*The metaphysical elements of justice*] (J. Ladd, Trans.). Indianapolis: Bobbs-Merrill, 1965. (Originally published, 1797.)

Lamm, H., & Myers, D. G. Group-induced polarization of attitude and behavior. In L. Berkowitz (Ed.), *Advances in experimental social psychology* (Vol. 2). New York: Academic Press, 1978.

Lempert, R. O. Civil juries and complex cases: Let's not rush to judgment. *Michigan Law Review,* 1981, *80,* 68–132.

Lipton, D., Martinson, R., and Wilks, J. *The effectiveness of correctional treatment: A survey of treatment evaluation studies.* New York: Praeger, 1975.

McFatter, R. M. Sentencing strategies and justice: Effects of punishment philosophy on sentencing decisions. *Journal of Personality and Social Psychology,* 1978, *36,* 1490–1500.

Meehl, P. E. *Clinical versus statistical prediction: A theoretical analysis and review of the literature.* Minneapolis: University of Minnesota Press, 1954.

Monahan, J., & Loftus, E. The psychology of law. *Annual Review of Psychology,* 1982, *33,* 441–475.

Munsterberg, H. *On the witness stand: Essays on psychology and crime*. New York: Doubleday, 1915.

Parker v. North Carolina, 397 U.S. 790 (1970).

Rich, W. D., Sutton, P. L., Clear, T. D., & Saks, M. J. *Sentencing guidelines: Their operation and impact on the courts*. Williamsburg, Va.: National Center for State Courts, 1981.

Saks, M. J. Ignorance of science is no excuse. *Trial*, 1974, *10*, 18ff.

Saks, M. J. The limits of scientific jury selection: Ethical and empirical. *Jurimetrics Journal*, 1976, *17*, 3–22.

Saks, M. J. *Jury verdicts*. Lexington, Mass.: Heath, 1977.

Saks, M. J., & Hastie, R. *Social psychology in court*. New York: Van Nostrand Reinhold, 1978.

Sawyer, J. Measurement and prediction, clinical and statistical. *Psychological Bulletin*, 1966, *66*, 178–200.

Schulman, J., Shaver, P., Colman, R., Enrich, B., and Christie, R. Recipe for a jury. *Psychology Today*, 1973, *6*, 37.

Schum, D. A., & Martin, A. W. An introduction to formal and empirical research on cascaded inference in jurisprudence. *Law and Society Review*, 1982, *17*, 105–151.

Severance, L. J., & Loftus, E. Improving the ability of jurors to comprehend and apply criminal jury instructions. *Law and Society Review*, 1982, *17*, 153–197.

Spitzer, R. J., Forman, J., & Nee, J. DSM-III Field Trials: Initial interrater diagnostic reliability. *American Journal of Psychiatry*, 1979, *136*, 815–817.

Stephenson, G. M., & Brotherton, C. J. Social progression and polarization: A study of discussion and negotiation in group mining supervisors. *British Journal of Social and Clinical Psychology*, 1975, *14*, 241–252.

Thomas, D. A. *Principles of sentencing*. London: Heinemann, 1979.

Thomsen. Sentencing in income tax cases. *Federal Probation*, 1962, *26*, 10.

Uhrbrock, R. S. The personnel interview. *Personnel Psychology*, 1948, *1*, 273–302.

von Hirsch, A. *Doing justice: The choice of punishments*. New York: Hill and Wang, 1976.

Weiner, B. Achievement motivation as conceptualized by an attribution theorist. In B. Weiner (Ed.), *Achievement motivation and attribution theory*. Morristown, N.J.: General Learning Press, 1974.

Williams v. Florida, 399 U.S. 78 (1970).

Zeisel, H. ". . . and then there were none." The diminution of the federal jury. *The University of Chicago Law Review*, 1971, *38*, 710–724.

Zeisel, H., & Diamond, S. S. Convincing empirical evidence on the six-member jury. *University of Chicago Law Review*, 1974, *41*, 281–295.

Zeisel, H., & Diamond, S. S. The search for sentencing equity: Sentence review in Massachusetts and Connecticut. *American Bar Foundation Research Journal*, 1977, *4*, 883–940.

Zeisel, H., & Diamond, S. S. The effect of peremptory challenges on jury and verdict: An experiment in a Federal District Court. *Stanford Law Review*, 1978, *30*, 491–530.

JOHN MONAHAN

THE PREDICTION OF VIOLENT BEHAVIOR: DEVELOPMENTS IN PSYCHOLOGY AND LAW

J ohn Monahan is professor of law, psychology, and legal medicine at the University of Virginia Law School. He is also associate director of the university's Institute of Law, Psychiatry, and Public Policy. After receiving his PhD in clinical psychology from Indiana University in 1972, he taught at the University of California, Irvine.

Monahan has been a fellow in law and psychology at the Harvard and Stanford Law Schools and a member of the Panel on Legal Issues of the President's Commission on Mental Health and the Panel on Offender Rehabilitation of the National Academy of Sciences. He is the founding president of the American Psychological Association's Division of Psychology and Law. With Elizabeth Loftus he wrote the chapter "The Psychology of Law" for the 1982 *Annual Review of Psychology.*

Monahan has testified before congressional committees on matters of mental health and criminal justice policy; his work in this area has been cited in decisions of the U.S. Supreme Court and other judicial bodies. His most recent book is *The Clinical Prediction of Violent Behavior,* which won the 1982 Manfred Guttmacher Award of the American Psychiatric Association.

JOHN MONAHAN

THE PREDICTION OF VIOLENT BEHAVIOR: DEVELOPMENTS IN PSYCHOLOGY AND LAW

D espite William James's admonition that we should not try to write biographies in advance, much law is premised on the belief that we can. In child custody cases the issue often is who will be the better parent. In wrongful death suits the question is how long the deceased would have been expected to earn a living had he or she not been killed.

The prediction of one particular form of behavior is the subject of intense legal interest. Forecasting and therefore preventing violent or dangerous behavior play a central role in a wide variety of legal decisions dealing with institutionalization in a prison or mental hospital and length of confinement. Psychologists have been intimately involved with these decisions as advisors to the courts and often as the de facto decision makers themselves.

In this paper I intend to (1) address the controversies that surround the psychological prediction of violence; (2) discuss the research that has occasioned these controversies and the policy changes that the research has provoked; (3) describe recent developments in violence prediction and their implications for policy change; and (4) speculate on

Parts of the first two sections of this paper are adapted from my monograph, *The Clinical Prediction of Violent Behavior* (1981). Parts of the last two sections are adapted from the 1982 Manfred Guttmacher Lecture to the American Psychiatric Association, "The Prediction of Violent Behavior: Toward a Second Generation of Theory and Policy" (Monahan, in press).

the research and policy directions that are likely to confront the field in the foreseeable future.

The Current Controversies

The law has always relied at least implicitly on predictions of harm. Vagrancy statutes, for example, were largely based on the intuitive notion that people who loiter where they have no reason to be are likely to cause "trouble." As predictions of harm became more explicitly codified, their role in the legal process became more closely scrutinized. Since the early 1970s, that scrutiny has concentrated on charges that predictions of violence are deficient in three respects: empirical, political, and professional (Monahan, 1981).

The Empirical Attack: Accurate Prediction Is Impossible

Rarely have research data been as quickly or almost universally accepted by the academic and professional communities as those supporting the proposition that mental health professionals are highly inaccurate at predicting violent behavior. We shall consider prediction research in more detail shortly, but the reader should be forewarned that stock in the predictive enterprise is going very cheaply.

A task force of the American Psychiatric Association concluded that "the state of the art regarding predictions of violence is very unsatisfactory. The ability of psychiatrists or any other professionals to reliably predict future violence is unproved" (1974, p. 30). In 1978, a task force of the American Psychological Association reached a similar conclusion:

> It does appear from reading the research that the validity of psychological predictions of dangerous behavior, at least in the sentencing and release situation we are considering, is extremely poor, so poor that one could oppose their use on the strictly empirical grounds that psychologists are not professionally competent to make such judgments. (p. 1110)

The latest edition of the American Civil Liberties Union (ACLU) handbook, *The Rights of Mental Patients* (Ennis & Emery, 1978), states that "it now seems beyond dispute that mental health professionals have *no* expertise in predicting future dangerous behavior either to self or others. In fact, predictions of dangerous behavior are wrong about 95 percent of the time" (p. 20; italics in original).

Kahle and Sales (1980) surveyed several hundred practicing psychiatrists, clinical psychologists, and mental health lawyers in a national study of attitudes toward civil commitment. They asked the respondents to estimate the "percentage of accurate predictions which are made with current methods of predicting dangerousness to others" (p. 279). The groups did not differ significantly; the mean estimates of predictive accuracy were 40 percent to 46 percent.

The Political Attack: Prediction Violates Civil Liberties

Originally voiced by Szasz, the position that preventive or therapeutic intervention based on a prediction of behavior violates the most fundamental rights guaranteed in a democratic society—punishment for past acts, not detention for future acts—has gained a large number of adherents. Indeed, the very designation of an act as dangerous or violent reflects political values that some may find unacceptable.

> Drunken drivers are dangerous both to themselves and to others. They injure and kill many more people than, for example, persons with paranoid delusions of persecution. Yet, people labeled "paranoid" are readily committable, while drunken drivers are not. Some types of dangerous behavior are even rewarded. Race-car drivers, trapeze artists, and astronauts receive admiration and applause. In contrast, the poly-surgical addict and the would-be suicide receive nothing but contempt and aggression. Indeed, the latter type of dangerousness is considered a good cause for commitment. Thus, it is not dangerousness in general that is at issue here, but rather the manner in which one is dangerous. (Szasz, 1963, p. 46)

The most recent frontal political assault on the use of predictions of violent behavior occurred in the context of criminal sentencing. The "just deserts" mode of imprisonment, which has been adopted by many states, explicitly eschews reliance on predictive considerations in determining an offender's release from prison (von Hirsch, 1976; Twentieth Century Fund, 1976). In its place is an explicitly normative and moral judgment of relative harm and the offender's culpability for having committed it.

> Predictive restraint poses special ethical problems. The fact that the person's liberty is at stake reduces the moral acceptability of mistakes of overprediction. Moreover, one may question whether it is ever just to *punish* someone more severely for what he is expected to do, even if the prediction was accurate. (von Hirsch, 1976, p. 26, italics in original)

The Professional Attack: Prediction Destroys the Helping Role

After mental health professionals have been blasted for years as empirically incompetent to predict violent behavior and as cryptofascists if they tried, some practitioners have counterattacked. They not only have outflanked their critics by *agreeing* that accurate prediction is factually impossible and politically improper but also have gone them one better by asserting that the prediction of violence and subsequent interventions to avert it are not—and in fact never were—within the purview of the mental health professions. Further, it was the legal system that asked the psychiatrist and psychologist to give opinions regarding violence potential for use in civil commitment and other proceedings. If mental health professionals naively acquiesced, they have now discovered that this incursion into forecasting was a mistake. It was a mistake not simply because research allegedly showed the effort to be fruitless or because political rights were trampled but because in the process the mental health professional surrendered the essential role as a healer of psychic pain and became an agent of social control.

The professional attack on prediction was led by Alan Stone in his highly influential monograph, *Mental Health and the Law: A System in Transition* (1975). Stone proposed a new medical model of civil commitment, openly based on paternalistic concern for the patient's welfare rather than on concern for society's protection. His thank-you theory "divests civil commitment of a police function; dangerous behavior is returned to the province of the criminal law. Only someone who is irrational, treatable, and incidentally dangerous would be confined to the mental health system" (p. 70).

Even if accurate prediction could be accomplished with civil liberties safeguarded, many mental health professionals would still oppose participating in any scheme that would make them agents of social control rather than benefactors of the individual client.

The Existing Research Base

Outcome Studies of Clinical Prediction

At least five studies published since 1972 have attempted to validate the ability of psychiatrists and psychologists to predict violent behavior. Kozol, Boucher, and Garofalo (1972) reported a 10-year study involving 592 male offenders; most of them had been convicted of violent sex crimes. At the Massachusetts Center for the Diagnosis and Treatment of Dangerous Persons, each offender was examined independently by at least two psychiatrists, two psychologists, and a social worker. These clinical examinations, along with a full psychological test battery and "a meticulous reconstruction of the life history elicited from multiple sources—the patient himself, his family, friends, neighbors, teachers, employers, and court, correctional and mental hospital record" (p. 383) —formed the data base for their predictions.

Of the 592 patients admitted to the facility for diagnostic observation, 435 were released. Kozol et al. recommended the release of 386 as nondangerous and opposed the release of 49 as dangerous (the court decided otherwise). During the 5-year follow-up period, 8 percent of those predicted as not dangerous became recidivists by committing a serious assaultive act, and 34.7 percent of those predicted as dangerous committed such an act.

Although the assessment of dangerousness by Kozol and his colleagues appears to have some validity, the problem of false positives stands out. Sixty-five percent of the individuals identified as dangerous did not in fact commit a dangerous act. Despite the extensive examining, testing, and data gathering that they undertook, Kozol et al. were wrong in two of every three predictions of discovered violence (cf., Monahan, 1973; Kozol, Boucher, & Garofalo, 1973).

The Patuxent Institution in Maryland has a purpose similar to that of the Massachusetts Center. Data are available on its first 10 years of operation (State of Maryland, 1973). Four hundred twenty-one patients, each with at least 3 years of treatment at Patuxent, were considered. The psychiatric staff opposed the release of 286 of these patients on the grounds that they were still dangerous (the court released them anyway). The staff recommended the release of 135 patients as safe (the court concurred). The criterion was any new offense (not necessarily violent) appearing on the Federal Bureau of Investigation (FBI) reports of ex-patients during the first 3 years after their release.

Of those patients released by the court against staff advice, the recidivism rate was 46 percent for patients released directly from the hospital and 39 percent for those with a "conditional release experience." Of those patients released on the staff's recommendation and continued for outpatient treatment on parole, 7 percent recidivated. Thus, after at least 3 years of observation and treatment, 54 percent to 61 percent of the patients predicted by the staff as dangerous actually were found to be safe. As with the Kozol et al. (1972) study, some predictive validity does seem to accrue to the predictions (7 percent recidivism, compared with 39 percent to 46 percent recidivism). Still, the majority of those patients predicted as dangerous were actually not discovered to be criminal in any sense.

A more recent and much more sophisticated evaluation of Patuxent by Steadman (1977) concluded that "the rearrest rate for both violent offenses and all offenses of all those released to the street with Patuxent approval vary much less from those of all relevant comparison groups than prior reports have demonstrated" (p. 206). For example, the arrest rate for *violent* crime over a 3-year period for those inmates recommended by the staff for release (i.e., those predicted as not dangerous) was 31 percent, whereas the comparable rate for those predicted as violent by the staff but released by the court was 41 percent. This 10-percent difference between the groups predicted as violent and as safe is much more modest than the 32-percent to 39-percent difference claimed in the earlier research. (See Gordon, 1977, for a contrasting view of this study.) Partially because of these new research findings, the Maryland legislature has abolished the defective delinquent statute under which the Patuxent program operated.

A U.S. Supreme Court decision in 1966 provided another aspect for study. The Court held that Johnnie Baxstrom had been denied equal protection of the law by being detained beyond his maximum prison sentence in an institution for the criminally insane without the benefit of a new hearing to determine his current dangerousness (*Baxstrom v. Herold,* 1966). While in prison Baxstrom was diagnosed as mentally disordered and transferred to a hospital for the criminally insane, where he was kept past the expiration date of his sentence. The court ruled that he must be released or at least granted a civil commitment hearing, at which the state would have to prove his dangerousness. The ruling resulted in the transfer of nearly 1,000 persons "reputed to be some of the most dangerous mental patients in the state [of New York]" from hospitals for the criminally insane to civil mental hospitals (Steadman, 1972). This transfer provided an excellent opportunity for naturalistic research on the validity of the psychiatric predictions of dangerousness, on which the extended detentions were based.

There has been an extensive follow-up program on the Baxstrom patients (Steadman & Cocozza, 1974). Researchers found that the level of violence experienced in the civil mental hospitals was much less than had been feared, that the civil hospitals adapted well to the massive transfer of patients, and that the Baxstrom patients were treated the same as the civil patients. Only 20 percent of the Baxstrom patients were assaultive to persons in the civil hospital or the community at any time during the 4 years following their transfer. Furthermore, only 3 percent of the Baxstrom patients were sufficiently dangerous to be returned to a hospital for the criminally insane during the 4 years after the decision (Steadman & Halfon, 1971). Steadman and Keveles (1972) followed 121 Baxstrom patients who had been released into the community (i.e., discharged from both the criminal and civil mental hospitals). During an average of 2½ years of freedom, only 9 of the 121 patients (8 percent) were convicted of a crime; only one of those convictions was for a violent act.

The Supreme Court's Baxstrom decision prompted a similar group of "mentally disordered offenders" in Pennsylvania to petition successfully for release (*Dixon v. Pennsylvania,* 1971). The results of the subsequent release of 438 patients have been reported by Thornberry and

Jacoby (1979) and are remarkably similar to those reported by Steadman. Only 14 percent of the former patients were discovered to have engaged in behaviors injurious to other persons during the 4 years after their release.

Finally, Cocozza and Steadman (1976) followed 257 indicted felony defendants who were found incompetent to stand trial in New York State in 1971 and 1972. All defendants were examined for a determination of dangerousness by two psychiatrists, with 60 percent predicted as dangerous and 40 percent not dangerous. Subjects were followed in the hospital and in the community for a 3-year period. Although those predicted as dangerous were slightly but insignificantly more likely to be assaultive during their initial incompetency hospitalization than those predicted as not dangerous (42 percent compared with 36 percent), this relationship was reversed for those rearrested for a crime after their release, with 49 percent of the dangerous group and 54 percent of the not-dangerous group rearrested. Predictive accuracy was poorest in the case of a rearrest for a violent crime, "perhaps the single most important indicator of the success of the psychiatric predictions." Only 14 percent of the dangerous group, compared with 16 percent of the not-dangerous group, were rearrested for violent offenses. Although these data are susceptible to alternative interpretations involving the possibly confounding effects of treatment received during hospitalization (Monahan, 1978), the authors believe that they constitute "the most definitive evidence available on the lack of expertise and accuracy of psychiatric predictions of dangerousness" and indeed represent "clear and convincing evidence of the inability of psychiatrists or of anyone else to accurately predict dangerousness" (p. 1101).

If one takes into account that the 46 percent true positive rate reported in the first Patuxent study refers to *any* crimes, not necessarily violent ones, and discounts that figure accordingly, it would be fair to conclude that the "best" clinical research indicates that psychiatrists and psychologists are accurate in no more than one of three predictions of violent behavior over a several-year period among institutionalized populations who both had committed violence (and thus had high base rates for it) and were diagnosed as mentally ill.

Criticisms of Prediction Research

The strongest criticism of the existing prediction research is that it severely underestimates the extent of violent behavior committed by the individuals predicted as violent, and thus many of those claimed as false positives are actually true positives who have not yet been caught. To the extent that this argument is valid, it seriously undercuts the thrust of the research findings. There is no question that *some* underestimations of violence occurred in the research. The question is how much, so that a correction factor can be applied to the data obtained. Let us consider the problem in detail.

Each of the clinical prediction studies relied primarily on *arrest* for a violent crime as its criterion. The Steadman studies included institutional assault and civil commitment for dangerousness along with arrest; Thornberry and Jacoby (1979) included civil commitment based on a dangerous act. How accurate an estimate of *violent behavior* is arrest for a violent crime, even if augmented by these other measures?

According to the National Victimization Panel (Department of Justice, 1978)—a national study in which an interviewer inquired whether a citizen had been the victim of a crime in the past year—only 47 percent of those who stated that they had been the victim of a violent crime reported the act to the police. In other words 53 percent of the violent crimes reported to the interviewer were not reported to the police. For several reasons this dramatic figure appears somewhat inflated. Citizens who said that they had not reported their victimization were asked the reason for not reporting. Twenty percent said that the act was "not serious enough" to report. Three percent said that it was "too inconvenient" to fill out a police form. Nineteen percent gave no classifiable reason for not reporting. As Levine (1976) has noted:

> Many trivial grievances which stay out of police records because people are not very upset are elevated to criminal status by the aggressive probing and searching of interviewers. . . . Since survey findings seem to include many of these trivial occurrences, the results are highly skewed and give an unrealistically grim portrayal of the crime problem. (p. 317)

If one discounts those violent "crimes" that victims themselves believe are trivial, a reasonable estimate might be that two of every three violent crimes committed in the United States are reported to the police (cf. Levine, 1976).

What is done about the violent crime that is reported? The most recent FBI statistics (Webster, 1978) reveal that approximately one-half of reported violent crime is cleared by an arrest. One could conclude, therefore, that two of every three violent crimes in the United States are reported to the police; of these, one results in an arrest.

In terms of the criterion problem in prediction research, one could argue that because only one-third of violent crime results in an arrest, it is hardly surprising that the best prediction studies can show only a one-third accuracy rate in predicting arrest. How could it be otherwise, since two-thirds of the criterion is hidden? Indeed, if one corrected for unreported and unsolved violent crime by multiplying the true-positive rate by a factor of 3, then the best prediction studies, instead of being only one-third accurate, are in fact *perfectly accurate* in predicting arrest for violent behavior.

Several factors weigh heavily against such a large correction factor. The difficulty in this argument lies in the assumption that violent behavior is evenly distributed among the population being predicted. If this were so—if, for example, each person predicted as violent actually committed one violent act—then a one-third accuracy rate in predicting arrest, which itself is only one-third accurate in estimating violent behavior, would amount to virtually flawless prediction. There is much reason, however, to believe that violent behavior is far from evenly distributed.

Wolfgang (1978) interviewed a sample of the subjects in his Philadelphia cohort study. Offenders reported committing a mean of three injury offenses for each arrest for an injury offense, with recidivists (those arrested between two and four times) reporting more than seven injury offenses per arrest. Likewise, the Rand study of habitual offenders (Petersilia, Greenwood, & Lavin, 1977) found that offenders reported committing 10 felonies per arrest. If we accepted Wolfgang's figure of three violent acts per each arrest and used it to correct for the proportion of actual violence accounted for by those people arrested for violent crime, we would conclude that *all* violent crime is committed by those people who are eventually arrested for it.

Data such as those of Wolfgang and Petersilia would support the argument that the one-third of the individuals who are predicted as violent and are arrested for a violent crime are in fact the same people who commit most of the unreported and unsolved violent acts. It is not that the false positives are really true positives in disguise but rather that the true positives are "truer" (i.e., more violent) than we imagined. As Shinnar and Shinnar (1975, p. 597) have stated: "The important question is who commits the 70 percent of crimes which are never solved. . . . [T]he most likely possibility is that they are committed by the same group of recidivists who commit the 30 percent of crimes which are solved."

What, then, are we to make of the criticism that using number of arrests severely underestimates the number of people who commit violent acts and thus greatly inflates the number of false positives? Obviously some of the unreported and unsolved violence is committed by persons who have escaped detection and are thus mislabeled. Obviously, too, some of the people who have been apprehended and have thus validated the accuracy of a prediction have committed more violence than that ascribed to them. Pending future research and in light of the findings of Wolfgang (1978), Petersilia et al. (1977), and Shinnar and Shinnar (1977), I would offer the conclusion that current prediction studies provide *reasonably accurate estimates* of the validity of clinical predictions of violence, at least among populations of people who have high base rates for violence because they have already committed violence.

Related Bodies of Research

One other body of research is often cited as relevant to the topic of prediction: the epidemiologic research on the relationship between crime and mental disorder. To the extent that mental disorder puts one at increased actuarial risk of committing a violent crime, the argument goes, violence should be easier to predict in mentally disordered persons. The justification for the involuntary commitment of the mentally disordered and for the near-automatic commitment of persons acquitted of crime by reason of insanity often invokes this reasoning.

Mental illness and violent behavior have always been linked in popular belief. Brydall, writing in 1700, traced the roots of civil commitment of the mentally ill in England to "the old Roman law" that provided that "Guards or Keepers be appointed for Madmen not only to look that they do not mischief to themselves, but also that they be not destructive to others" (quoted in Dershowitz, 1974). After Daniel M'Naghten was acquitted by reason of insanity in 1843, the *Times* of London published this ditty (quoted in Greenland, 1978):

> Ye people of England exult and be glad
> For ye're now at the mercy of the merciless mad.

The first mental hospital in the American colonies was founded at the urging of Benjamin Franklin, who relied heavily on the argument that the mentally ill were prone to violence. In his petition to the Pennsylvania Assembly he claimed

> That with the Numbers of People, the Number of Persons distempered in Mind and deprived of their rational Faculties, has greatly increased in this province; That some of them going at large are a terror to their neighbours, who are daily apprehensive of the Violences they may commit. (quoted in Monahan & Geis, 1976, p. 146)

Likewise, the modern public correlates violence and mental illness, in no small part because of a systematic exaggeration by the media of the crime rates of the mentally ill (Steadman & Cocozza, 1978).

There is a growing and converging body of empirical research on the relation between violence and mental illness. The research addresses two questions: (1) What is the prevalence of psychiatric disorder among prison populations? and (2) What is the violent crime rate of people released from mental hospitals? Although answers to these questions will not provide an entirely satisfactory account of the relationship between violent behavior and mental disorder, because a large portion of diagnosably disordered persons have never been in mental hospitals and a large portion of violent offenders successfully avoid prison, the answers do provide a useful antidote to popular mythology.

Bolton (1976) reported the results of a psychiatric epidemiological survey of inmates of adult jails and juvenile detention facilities in five California counties. Over 1,000 adult offenders and 650 juveniles were examined. He reported that 6.7 percent of the adults and 2.9 percent of the juveniles were diagnosed as psychotic; 9.3 percent of the adults and 20.6 percent of the juveniles were found to have a nonpsychotic mental disorder. Personality disorders were reported for 21.0 percent of the adults and for 25.2 percent of the juveniles. Monahan, Caldeira, and Friedlander (1979) found police estimates that 30 percent of the persons arrested are at least somewhat mentally ill but only 12 percent are either moderately or severely mentally ill. Roth and Ervin (1971, p. 429) concluded that "psychiatric morbidity in criminal populations is probably somewhere between 15 and 20 percent."

Considering that the President's Commission on Mental Health (1978, p. 8) recently concluded that "as many as 25 percent of the population are estimated to suffer . . . emotional disorders at any time" and given that the social classes from which street offenders are drawn are disproportionately represented in that figure, the findings of Bolton (1976), Monahan et al. (1979), and Roth and Ervin (1971) do not indicate an increased rate of mental illness among jail inmates.

The most comprehensive study of rates of psychiatric disorder among offender populations has been performed by Guze (1976). Guze's review of the literature is representative of the conclusions of others (e.g., Brodsky, 1973).

> Overall, the other studies may be summarized as follows. Psychosis, schizophrenia, primary affective disorders, and the various neurotic disorders are seen in only a minority of identified criminals. There is no complete agreement as to whether any of these conditions is more common among criminals than the general population, but it is clear that these disorders carry only a *slightly* increased risk of criminality if any at all. (Guze, pp. 35–36, italics in original)

Guze's own study of 223 male and 66 female felons in Missouri arrived at the following findings:

> Sociopathy, alcoholism, and drug dependence are the psychiatric disorders characteristically associated with serious crime. Schizophrenia, primary affective disorders, anxiety neurosis, obsessional neurosis, phobic neurosis, and brain syndromes are not. Sexual deviations, defined as illegal *per se,* are not, in the absence of accompanying sociopathy, alcoholism, and drug dependence, associated with other serious crime.

Diamond (1974), commenting on Guze's earlier work, noted that sociopathy, alcoholism, and drug dependence "are precisely those psychiatric states which are less easily definable and less generally agreed to be illnesses at all" (p. 448). Indeed, Guze defined *sociopathy* for the purposes of his research as follows:

> This diagnosis was made if at least two of the following five manifestations were present in addition to a history of police trouble (other than traffic offenses): a history of excessive fighting . . . school delinquency . . . a poor job record . . . [or] a period of wanderlust or being a runaway. . . . For women, a history of prostitution could be substituted for one of the five manifestations. (p. 35)

If all prostitutes who have ever been truant in school or all unemployed males with a period of wanderlust in their history are counted as sociopaths, it is not difficult to understand why 78 percent of all male and 65 percent of all female felons were so diagnosed.

Therefore, with the exception of a higher prevalence of the disorders of alcoholism and drug dependence, prisoners do not appear to have higher rates of diagnosable mental illness than their class-matched peers in the open community.

An interesting pattern exists in the data on violent crime rates of former mental patients. Almost without exception, studies in the 1950s and earlier found that released patients had a *lower* rate of arrest for violent behavior than the general population (e.g., Brill & Malzberg, 1954), while studies in the 1960s and 1970s have consistently found a *higher* rate of violent behavior among former patients than among the nonpatient population (e.g., Zitrin, Hardesty, Burdock, & Drosaman, 1976). What accounts for this wholesale shift in the research findings?

According to Cocozza, Melick, and Steadman (1978), the apparently increased crime rate among former patients reflects "the changing clientele of state hospitals." The researchers examined the arrest records of almost 4,000 patients released from New York State mental hospitals in 1968 and 1975, using a 19-month follow-up period. They paid particular attention to whether the former patient had ever been arrested before hospitalization.

A striking pattern emerges. Although it is true that former patients as a group do have a substantially higher arrest record for all types of crime than does the general population, patients without an arrest record *before* hospitalization have a *lower* arrest rate than the general population has. Patients with *one* arrest before hospitalization have a slightly higher than average arrest rate for violent crime once they are released. Patients with *two or more* prior arrests have a drastically higher violent crime rate than that of the general population. Thus, compared with the general population, the higher rate of violent crime committed by released mental patients can be accounted for entirely by those patients with a record, particularly an extensive record, of criminal activity before their hospitalization. This finding is consistent with the literature on violent crime among criminal populations: A record of past violence is the best predictor of future violence.

What has caused the *increase* in violent crime rates among released patients in recent years? Steadman, Cocozza, and Melick (1978) compared their findings with those reported by Brill and Malzberg (1954) on a comparable population of New York patients released in 1947. The results of the two studies are almost identical except that only 15 percent of the 1947 patients had a prior arrest record whereas 40 percent of the 1975 subjects did. As Brill and Malzberg noted 25 years ago:

> Arrests in the ex-mental hospital patients were largely concentrated in a relatively small, rather well-demarcated group of persons with a previous criminal record, and their anti-social behavior was clearly correlated with well-known factors which operate in the general population and was not correlated with the factors of mental illness except in a negative way . . . [An] attack of mental illness with hospitalization does not tend to leave an inclination toward criminal activity greater than that which existed prior to the illness and . . . does not produce such a tendency if it did not previously exist. . . . (pp. 12–13)

Rabkin (1979, p. 25) came to a similar conclusion in her exhaustive review of every study published on the topic:

> At the present time there is no evidence that [released patients'] mental status as such raises their arrest risk; rather, antisocial behavior and mentally ill behavior apparently coexist, particularly among young, unmarried, unskilled poor males, especially those belonging to ethnic minorities.

The real issue, therefore, is not what psychological factors account for the increased crime rate among released mental patients but rather what sociological and economic factors underlie the administrative and political decision to send more criminals to mental hospitals in the first place. As chronic-geriatric patients—who have a very low crime rate— are being "deinstitutionalized" from mental hospitals into nursing homes, the proportion of beds that are being filled by younger and more violent persons—who in the past might have been sent to jail or prison (Stone, 1975)—is rising. As Steadman et al. (1978, p. 820) have noted, "if one were to gather a group of men of whom 40 percent had previously been arrested, from the general population, it is quite likely that the arrest rates found among the 1975 former patient group would be duplicated or exceeded." (Cf. Sosowsky, 1980. This research area is reviewed in Monahan & Steadman, 1983, pp. 145–188.)

There is one interpretation of these data against which I wish fervently to guard. The research looks at rates of criminal behavior among *groups* of prisoners and rates of mental disorder among *groups* of mental patients. The research has not sought to examine the relation between crime and mental disorder within any given *individual* in those groups. One must not commit the "ecological fallacy" in reverse. From a finding that there is no relation between crime and mental disorder in the aggregate, one cannot infer that persons who are both criminal and mentally disordered do not exist. Even if there were no relation whatever between group rates of criminal behavior and group rates of mental disorder, one would expect the distributions to overlap at chance levels. That is, if X percent of a given population were mentally disordered and there were *no* relation between mental disorder and criminal behavior, one would still expect X percent of the criminal population to be mentally disordered.

It is conceptually difficult, and often legally impossible, to address the existence of criminal behavior and mental disorder within the same individuals without invoking the concept of *causality*. The legal question, as in the insanity defense, is usually phrased as whether the criminal behavior was a result of the mental disorder. One of three relationships between crime and mental disorder may exist in given individuals: (1) Mental disorder may simply *coexist* with criminality without any causal significance, much as an offender may have a toothache without arousing suspicions of dental determinism; (2) mental disorder may *predispose* one toward criminality, as in the case of M'Naghten's delusion that he was the victim of persecution by the prime minister of England; and (3) mental disorder may *inhibit* criminality, as catatonia would inhibit a person otherwise inclined toward rape.

There can be little doubt that some people fit each of these causal paths. The relative proportion of persons who fit each path is unknown. From the general pattern of the data reviewed here, however, one might infer that paths 2 and 3—predisposing toward and inhibiting criminality—are of approximately equal frequency and therefore cancel out each other when aggregated into group rates.

In line with this reasoning, one would expect that providing effective psychiatric and psychological treatment to mentally disordered offenders would (1) have no effect on the criminal recidivism rate of those offenders whose mental disorder and criminal propensities merely coexist; (2) reduce the criminal recidivism rate of those offenders whose mental disorder predisposes them toward crime; and (3) increase the criminal recidivism rate of those offenders whose mental disorder inhibits crime. Only in the latter two groups, with mental disorder and criminal behavior causally related, would criminal recidivism be a relevant measure of treatment efficacy.

This is not to say that psychological technology can be effective in reducing the recidivism risk only of those offenders for whom mental disorder predisposes toward crime. However, if the effectiveness of therapeutic techniques is measured against the criterion of reduced criminal recidivism, those techniques should be targeted directly against recidivism, not against mental disorder as an intervening variable. There may, for example, be a small group of psychotic rapists for whom the cure of their psychosis will result in the cessation of their rapacious behavior. But there may also be a much larger group of non-psychotic rapists—or rapists whose psychosis and criminal tendencies coexist without being causally related—for whom psychological techniques aimed directly at reducing recidivism (e.g., training in self-control and socially appropriate forms of making sexual requests) would prove effective. The use of such techniques would leave intact any existing mental disorder.

Public Policy

This research on violence prediction had a significant effect on public policies. In the early 1970s, before such research findings became widely known, a national movement was afoot to revise the criteria for civil commitment away from an assessment of a need for treatment and toward a prediction of dangerousness to others or to self. So appealing to the legal mind was the libertarian logic of the dangerousness model that by the mid-1970s virtually every state had, if not entirely thrown over need for treatment in favor of dangerousness, at least grafted dangerousness onto its existing standards for commitment (Schwitzgebel and Schwitzgebel, 1980).

Also in the early 1970s, indeterminate prison sentences were the rule throughout much of the United States. A sentence could run from a brief minimum to a lengthy maximum—1 to 20 years, for example—and the decision about the release date was given to a parole board. These boards relied largely on their own intuitive clinical judgments, sometimes aided by psychological and psychiatric reports, to know the moment at which rehabilitation had been achieved and the offender could be released without danger.

These trends in mental health and criminal law were called into question by the research described on the prediction of violent behavior. Rarely has research been so uncritically accepted and so facilely generalized by both mental health professionals and lawyers as this first-generation research on the prediction of violence. The careful qualifications that the researchers placed on their findings and the circumscribed nature of the situations to which they might apply were forgotten in the rush to frame a bumper-sticker conclusion—"Psychiatrists and psychologists can't predict violence"—and paste it on every policy vehicle in sight.

Thus it was claimed that scientific research had conclusively demonstrated that reliance on predictions of dangerousness in involuntary commitment was—in my own unfortunate phrase—doomed (Monahan, 1976). Some took such dire assessments as empirical support for the policy conclusion at which they had already arrived on other grounds, namely, that involuntary hospitalization should be abolished (Szasz, 1977).

Others took this first-generation prediction research as empirical support not to end commitment but to change the criteria by which it was decided (e.g., Stone, 1975). In the debate between proponents of commitment standards based on dangerousness and commitment standards based on treatability, the prediction research became a weapon in the hands of the advocates of treatment. "Whatever the appropriate criterion is for civil commitment," they could say, "we know from research that it is not dangerousness."

As influential as this first-generation prediction research was in the mental health system, it had an even more profound impact on criminal justice. How could we send offenders to prison for indefinite periods in the belief that they would be released when they were safe, when prison psychologists, psychiatrists, and parole boards have shown little ability to distinguish the safe from the violent? Would it not be better to focus attention backward on the offender's moral blameworthiness in having chosen to commit crime in the first place, rather than forward on his or her likelihood of repeating the crime? Although many factors underlie the national move to abolish indeterminate prison sentences and to rehabilitate retribution as the guiding principle for allocating punishment, the research on the prediction of violent criminality has figured prominently among them (von Hirsch, 1975).

Second-Generation Research and Theory

In the past several years, what might be called a second generation of violence prediction research and theory, which casts these policy developments in a considerably different light, has begun to evolve (Monahan, in press). This second generation of scholarship on prediction has no rallying cry. If its bottom-line conclusion were put on a bumper sticker, it would read "Little is known about how accurately violent behavior can be predicted in many circumstances, but it may be possible to predict it accurately enough to be useful in some policy decisions."

Three Themes

There are three themes to this second generation of thought on violence prediction. The first concerns the limits of existing knowledge. Unquestionably a great deal can be learned from the existing research on prediction. But for a topic of such fundamental importance, the existing research base is remarkably shallow.

The most telling criticism concerns the scope of the existing prediction research. The studies deal with only one form of prediction—clinical prediction—and with only one setting for prediction—long-term custodial institutions. Other forms of prediction, emphasizing actuarial methods, and other settings for prediction, such as short-term community settings, have been largely unexplored. Yet it is precisely these other forms of and settings for prediction that are the most promising candidates for a workable level of predictive accuracy. The absence of evidence that violence can be validly predicted in some situations should not be construed as evidence of the absence of such validity.

The second and related theme of this new generation of thought on violence prediction involves a guarded optimism that some improvement in predictive accuracy is possible. For example, two studies published recently report true positive rates for the prediction of violent or assaultive behavior of 40 percent (where the base rate was 10 percent) and 41 percent (where the base rate was 8 percent). The first of these (State of Michigan, 1978) was an actuarial study of long-term parole prediction; the second (Rofman, Askinazi, and Fant, 1980), a short-term clinical study of civilly committed patients.

Care should be taken not to overstate this point. The study has yet to be done showing psychiatrists, psychologists, parole board members, or computers more often right than wrong in predicting violent behavior. But claims such as those of the American Civil Liberties Union (ACLU) (Ennis & Emery, 1978, p. 20) that mental health professionals are inaccurate "about 95 percent of the time" are simply untrue.

Finally, the second generation of scholarship on violence prediction is much more likely than its predecessor to evaluate public policies that rely on prediction in terms of *relative* rather than *absolute* moral and political values. There is a growing appreciation of the wisdom of Underwood's (1979) observation that "the assessment of predictive selection must take into account the nature of the plausible alternatives to predictive selection" (p. 1418).

Not only the uses of prediction determine its value. More fundamentally, moral and political assessments can be reached only when one takes into account how decisions that do *not* rely on prediction will be made. Here, recent policy developments should give us pause.

Just Deserts Sentencing

Consider, for example, the national movement toward determinate criminal sentencing based on what has come to be known as just deserts (von Hirsch, 1976). In its pure form, this model holds that the length of an offender's prison term should be based on two factors and two factors alone: the seriousness of the crime and the degree of the offender's moral culpability. Predictions of what an offender is likely to do when he or she leaves prison, the argument goes, should be of absolutely no relevance in deciding the length of the sentence. On the date of sentencing, an offender should know the date of release. Parole boards, along with their psychological consultants, would wither away. Indeed, in many states that have adopted determinate sentencing, the boards have already withered away.

As an abstract theory of sentencing, the just deserts model has many appealing attributes. It treats offenders as moral agents responsible for their own conduct, a stance likely to win the approval of Thomas Szasz. It promotes a more rational uniformity in sentencing. Best of all, it severs in one stroke the Gordian knot that utilitarian sentencing schemes based on predictions of recidivism have never been able to untangle: What factors are legitimate to rely on in forecasting crime? Can one, for example, rely on such socially sensitive but scientifically relevant factors as age and sex? The just deserts model simply disowns the problem by not making predictions at all.

Two problems have emerged, however, that make me wonder if we have not jumped from the frying pan of prediction into the fires of retribution. For one thing it is less clear than it should be how one goes about measuring what deserts are just deserts. With the prediction of criminal recidivism, at least the task was clear: Parole boards and psychiatrists and psychologists knew what they were supposed to do, even if they could not do it very well.

But how does one go about reliably assessing something as inherently subjective as moral culpability? If the prediction of recidivism is a Herculean task, then the assessment of culpability is a divine one. The primary imponderable in this area is whether one should take into account the pressures of society in influencing a person to commit a crime when measuring his or her culpability. Many would argue, for example, that the victims of poverty and discrimination have less free choice to commit crime and therefore should receive a shorter sentence than their more privileged accomplices (Gardiner, 1976). The principal counterpoint to this argument is that justice, in the largest sense of that term, requires that one consider not only the effects of sentencing on offenders for the crime that they have committed but also justice for the innocent people who will be the next victims of recidivists (Bedau, 1977). If one defines justice in this larger way, a concern with predicting recidivism becomes an integral part of the assessment of moral culpability, not an alternative to it.

The Rorschachlike murkiness of the concept of just deserts, however, is only one of its difficulties. More directly relevant to the concerns of mental health professionals is the real possibility that, having no sooner been thrown out of sentencing and parole hearings because the law of determinate sentencing has no place for their predictions of recidivism, psychiatrists and psychologists will quickly be recalled to assess factors that may mitigate moral culpability (Monahan & Ruggiero, 1980). Indeed, one of the principal reports that provided the impetus for determinate sentencing invites precisely this kind of mental health testimony. The report of the Twentieth Century Fund, *Fair and Certain Punishment,* lists the following statement as a factor that can reduce an offender's determinate sentence by up to 50 percent: "The defendant was suffering from a mental . . . condition that significantly reduced his culpability for the offense" (1976, p. 45).

Thus it would seem that the psychiatrists and psychologists precluded by the just deserts theory from offering their opinions on offenders' future dangerousness need not fear unemployment. The same theory will effectively require that they step up their activities in offering opinions on the moral culpability of offenders for past acts. Given the vagaries of assessing culpability, juries and judges may be receptive to any reference point that they can grasp, particularly one sounding scientific.

The problem is that if there is any mental health practice more controversial than the prediction of crime, it is the assessment of culpability for past crime. It will be ironic if all the problematic predictions of crime that the just deserts theory casts off are replaced by even more problematic psychiatric and psychological pronouncements about how much free will an offender had in the unsuccessful effort to resist temptation.

These three themes, then, characterize the second generation of research and theory on the prediction of violent behavior: We know less than we thought about the accuracy of predictions; what little we do know is not entirely bleak; and how useful this knowledge is depends on what we do with it, compared to what we would do without it.

Directions of Research and Policy

The immediate future of scholarship in violence prediction can be expected to continue these second-generation trends. We do not need more studies concluding that psychologists and psychiatrists are relatively inaccurate clinical predictors of whether mentally disordered offenders who have been institutionalized for lengthy periods will offend once more. There are so many nails in that coffin that we should declare the issue officially dead. Rather, what we need are, first, studies that vary the *methods* of prediction to focus on actuarial techniques, including those that incorporate clinical information in statistical tables and those that provide statistical tables to clinicians as an additional source on which to base clinical judgments; second, studies that vary the *factors* used in predictive decisions to include situational items, such as characteristics of the family environment, the work environment, and the peer group environment in which the individual is to function; and, third, studies that vary the *populations* on which predictive technology is brought to bear, to include short-term predictions made in the community. The report of the Twentieth Century Fund, Fair and Certain

Public policies implicating the prediction of violent behavior are unlikely to change much in the near future, at least as far as the mental health system is concerned. Even with California-type dangerousness standards, the vast majority of people being involuntarily hospitalized in this country are believed actively or passively dangerous to *themselves,* not to others. If dangerousness to others were completely abolished as a criterion for commitment—as some (Stone, 1975) advocate—it would make little difference in the number of people being committed (Monahan, Ruggiero and Friedlander, 1982).

The Concept of Liability

One public policy development regarding prediction, which began in the mental health system some time ago, is starting to move to other areas of law. The *Tarasoff* decision (1976) held psychiatrists and psychologists liable for civil damages when they "determine" or "pursuant to the standards of (their) profession should determine" that their patient poses a danger to others but fail to "use reasonable care to protect the intended victim." This vicarious liability rationale is being applied to a wide variety of other situations in which one party is allegedly in a position to predict that another party will be violent but does nothing to prevent the violent act or to warn others.

Recent cases have considered the liability of employers for the violent acts of their employees. Did they have reason to suspect that the employee would be violent? Was the employer negligent for failing to screen all job applicants with psychological tests or psychiatric interviews, e.g., for failing to assess the arson-prone personality in applicants for busboy positions in the hotel industry? Until the law is more settled in these areas, there may be something of a boom in psychiatric and psychological expert testimony on just when it is reasonable to expect nonprofessionals to predict violence or to call for professional assistance.

In the foreseeable future the real policy activity regarding dangerousness may be in the criminal justice system. The fact that the first task force commissioned by the current administration was the Attorney General's Task Force on Violent Crime (1981) is indicative of the topic's political priority. Two things underlie the criminal justice system's heightened commitment to focus its efforts on persons believed to be dangerous. The first is the realization from several sociological research projects, most notably the Philadelphia cohort study (Wolfgang, Figlio, & Sellin, 1972), that the majority of crime in this country is committed by a very small group of what are coming to be called high-rate criminal offenders. Wolfgang (1978), for example, found that 6 percent of the offenders in his study committed 54 percent of the crime. If we could somehow identify that 6 percent before they had a chance to perfect their criminal careers, it is argued, we would be well on our way to reducing the crime rate.

Limited Resources

The second factor determining the direction of research and policy is an acute awareness of the limits of the resources that society wishes to expend in controlling crime. There are not enough police officers to arrest everyone who commits a crime and not enough prosecutors and judges to try them if they were arrested. It would make little sense to prosecute all offenders to the extent allowed by law since there is surely no place in our bulging prisons to put them. Nor is there any indication that voters wish to tax themselves to provide the resources that a full-enforcement policy would require.

Thus the option of *selectively* applying the force of the criminal justice system takes on political appeal. Who should be selected to be the recipients of this full-court press but those high-rate offenders designated dangerous? Policies for concentrating police, prosecutorial, and prison resources on dangerous offenders are coming off the drawing boards and being presented to legislative committees (Greenwood, 1982). It is here that behavioral scientists, including psychiatrists and psychologists, are being called on. We are increasingly being asked to separate dangerous from nondangerous offenders.

Should these policy initiatives for selective incapacitation come to pass, I hope that our professions will have the wisdom to learn from their experience in making predictions regarding civil commitment and resist the temptation to utter conclusive judgments that this man or woman is dangerous. We should decline to launder for the legal system the social and demographic factors that anticipate crime and decline to let judges fob off on us the moral balancing of competing claims for the offender's freedom and the predicted victims' safety. We may be of some help in assessing the probability of violence, at least in some cases. But whether a person is dangerous "enough" to justify preventive confinement is not for us to say. That buck should stop at the judge's bench, not at the witness box.

The strategy that I would urge is to provide as much information to the legal system as possible regarding the prediction of violent behavior and then, within some broad moral constraints, to stand back and let the legal system do with it as it will. As one recent report on this topic stated, "Since it is not within the professional competence of psychologists [or psychiatrists] to offer conclusions on matters of law, psychologists [and psychiatrists] should resist pressure to offer such conclusions" (American Psychological Association, 1978, p. 1105).

Monahan and Wexler (1978, p. 38), in this regard, argue that when a mental health professional predicts that a person will be dangerous to others for the purpose of civil commitment, he or she is making three separate assertions:

1. The individual being examined has certain characteristics.
2. These characteristics are associated with a certain probability of violent behavior.
3. The probability of violent behavior is "sufficiently" great to justify preventive intervention.

The first two of these assertions, Monahan and Wexler hold, are professional judgments within the expertise of the mental health professional (judgments that can be challenged in court). The third is a social policy statement that must be arrived at through the political process and on which the mental health professional should have no more say than any other citizen (Morse, 1978). What the mental health professional should do, they argue, is present and defend an estimate of the probability that the individual will engage in violent behavior and leave to judges and legislators—who are the appropriate persons in a democratic society to weigh competing claims among social values—the decision as to whether this probability of violent behavior is sufficient to justify preventive interventions.

In no sense, for example, do the data on the prediction of violent behavior compel their own policy implications. Given that the level of predictive validity revealed in the research has been rather modest in an absolute sense, one could use the data to argue for across-the-board reductions in the length of institutionalization of prisoners and mental patients: Because we cannot be sure who will do us harm, we should detain no one. Alternatively, and with equal fervor and logic, one could use the same data to argue for across-the-board increases in the length of institutionalization: Because we cannot be sure which ones will be safe, we should detain them all. Whether a person uses the data in support of the first or the second of these implications will depend on how one assesses and weighs the various costs and benefits associated with each or on the nonutilitarian principles for allocating confinement that one adopts (e.g., Rawls, 1972). The principal impediment to developing straightforward cost/benefit ratios for predictive decision making is the lack of a common scale on which to order both costs and benefits (e.g., how are years in a prison or mental hospital to be compared with rapes, robberies, murders, or assaults prevented?).

Conclusion

There have been three generic attacks on psychiatrists and psychologists who offer predictions of an individual's violent behavior. To the first attack—that, as an empirical matter, violent behavior is simply impossible to predict—the second generation of research and theory on violence prediction offers some significant qualifications. The empirical foundation for the nihilist approach is less secure than many have believed.

To the second attack—that, as a political matter, prediction violates the essential liberties of persons who are the subjects of predictive assessments—the second generation of research and theory gives the same answer as the comedian Jack Benny, when asked if he liked his wife: "Compared to what?" But political evaluations of policies relying on prediction can be made only in the context of the feasible alternatives to prediction, alternatives that, experience is showing, are not the examplars of libertarian virtue that they once seemed.

What can we say about the final attack—that predicting dangerousness destroys the essential helping role of the mental health professions, that it turns psychiatrists and psychologists from healers of psychic pain into agents of social control? It seems that a rethinking of prediction also counsels that the strident rhetoric sometimes passing for rational discourse in this area be toned down. All human service professions have a social control component to them. Teachers, for example, whose role is to improve the welfare of their students, surely view themselves as transmitters of knowledge and culture. Yet they frequently function as disciplinarians, whose tasks include expelling those whose conduct is detrimental to the learning of others and acting as society's gatekeepers by withholding diplomas needed for jobs and further education from those who do not meet socially defined standards of academic performance. It is as the agents of society, not benefactors of the individual pupil, that teachers perform these functions.

Likewise, and more to the point, nonpsychiatric physicians perform a variety of social control functions with little adverse effect on their primary help-giving role. For instance, they can indicate the involuntary detention of persons who through no fault of their own carry contagious diseases. Also, they are bound in many states to report to the police whenever they suspect child abuse. Although one would hope that the community protection role of mental health professionals would be minimal relative to their helping functions (as with teachers and physicians), it does not seem unreasonable of society to ask that a limited social control function remain.

When sociologists use the term *social control,* they usually do so with a sneer. The image evoked is that of culturally or ideologically "different" people being punished when they deviate from middle-class norms. The government's real goal in controlling its citizens, according to the more colorful proponents of this perspective, is to turn everybody into clones of Donny and Marie Osmond.

But we are not talking in this context of psychology and psychiatry being manipulated to play an improper role in controlling more-or-less harmless deviations from social norms. We are talking of murder, rape, robbery, assault, and other forms of violent behavior. There is a widespread social consensus—a consensus that transcends political, racial, and economic groupings—that such activities tear at the already frayed social bonds that hold society together. When we lend professional assistance, however marginal, to improve society's control of those who will murder, rape, rob, and assault—provided that we do not let the nature of that assistance be overstated or distorted—we have nothing for which to apologize.

References

American Psychiatric Association. *Clinical aspects of the violent individual.* Washington, D.C.: Author, 1974.

American Psychological Association. Report of the Task Force on the Role of Psychology in the Criminal Justice System. *American Psychologist,* 1978, *33,* 1099–1113.

Attorney General's Task Force on Violent Crime: Final Report. Washington, D.C.: U.S. Government Printing Office, 1981.

Baxstrom v. Herold, 383 U.S. 107 (1966).

Bedau, H. Concessions to retribution in punishment. In J. Cederblom & W. Blizek (Eds.), *Justice and punishment.* Cambridge, Mass.: Ballinger, 1977.

Bolton, A. *A study of the need for and availability of mental health services for mentally disordered jail inmates and juveniles in detention facilities.* Unpublished report, Arthur Bolton Associates, Boston, 1976.

Brill, H., and Malzberg, B. *Statistical report on the arrest record of male ex-patients, age 16 and over, released from New York State mental hospitals during the period 1945–48.* Unpublished manuscript, New York State Department of Mental Hygiene, 1954.

Brodsky, S. *Psychologists in the criminal justice system.* Urbana: University of Illinois Press, 1973.

Cocozza, J., Melick, M., & Steadman, H. Trends in violent crime among ex-mental patients. *Criminology,* 1978, *16,* 317–334.

Cocozza, J., & Steadman, H. The failure of psychiatric predictions of dangerousness: Clear and convincing evidence. *Rutgers Law Review,* 1976, *29,* 1084–1101.

Department of Justice. *Criminal victimization in the United States.* Washington, D.C.: U.S. Government Printing Office, 1978.

Dershowitz, A. The origins of preventive confinement in Anglo-American law. Part I: The English experience. *University of Cincinnati Law Review,* 1974, *43,* 1–60.

Diamond, B. The psychiatric prediction of dangerousness. *University of Pennsylvania Law Review,* 1974, *123,* 439–452.

Dixon v. Pennsylvania, 325 F. Supp. 966 (1971).

Ennis, B., & Emery, R. *The rights of mental patients—An American Civil Liberties Union handbook.* New York: Avon, 1978.

Gardiner, M. The renaissance of retribution—An examination of doing justice. *Wisconsin Law Review,* 1976, *1976,* 781–815.

Gordon, R. A critique of the evaluation of Patuxent Institution, with particular attention to the issues of dangerousness and recidivism. *Bulletin of the American Academy of Psychiatry and the Law,* 1977, *5,* 210–255.

Greenland, C. *The prediction and management of dangerous behavior: Social policy issues.* Paper presented at the Law and Psychiatry Symposium, Clarke University, 1978.

Greenwood, P. The violent offender in the criminal justice system. In M. Wolfgang & N. Weiner (Eds.), *Criminal violence.* Beverly Hills: Sage, 1982.

Guze, S. *Criminality and psychiatric disorders.* New York: Oxford University Press, 1976.

Kahle, L., & Sales, B. Due process of law and the attitudes of professionals toward involuntary civil commitment. In P. Lipsitt & B. Sales (Eds.), *New directions in psycholegal research.* New York: Van Nostrand Reinhold, 1980.

Kozol, H., Boucher, R., & Garofalo, R. The diagnosis and treatment of dangerousness. *Crime and Delinquency,* 1972, *18,* 371–392.

Kozol, H., Boucher, R., & Garofalo, R. Dangerousness: A reply to Monahan. *Crime and Delinquency,* 1973, *19,* 554–555.

Levine, J. The potential for crime overreporting in criminal victimization surveys. *Criminology,* 1976, *14,* 307–330.

Monahan, J. Dangerous offenders: A critique of Kozol et al. *Crime and Delinquency,* 1973, *19,* 418–420.

Monahan, J. The prevention of violence. In J. Monahan (Ed.), *Community mental health and the criminal justice system.* New York: Pergamon Press, 1976.

Monahan, J. The prediction of violent criminal behavior: A methodological critique and prospectus. In A. Blumstein, J. Cohen, & D. Nagin (Eds.), *Deterrence and incapacitation: Estimating the effects of criminal sanctions on crime rates.* Washington, D.C.: National Academy of Sciences, 1978.

Monahan, J. *The clinical prediction of violent behavior.* Washington, D.C.: Government Printing Office, 1981.

Monahan, J. The prediction of violent behavior: Toward a second generation of theory and policy. *American Journal of Psychiatry,* in press.

Monahan, J., Caldeira, C., & Friedlander, H. The police and the mentally ill. A comparison of arrested and committed persons. *International Journal of Law and Psychiatry,* 1979, *2,* 509–518.

Monahan, J., & Geis, G. Controlling "dangerous" people. *Annals of the American Academy of Political and Social Science,* 1976, *423,* 142–151.

Monahan, J., & Ruggiero, M. Psychological and psychiatric aspects of determinate criminal sentencing. *International Journal of Law and Psychiatry,* 1980, *3,* 105–116.

Monahan, J., Ruggiero, M., & Friedlander, H. The Stone-Roth model of civil commitment and the California dangerousness standard: An operational comparison. *Archives of General Psychiatry,* 1982, *39,* 1267–1271.

Monahan, J., & Steadman, H. Crime and mental disorder. An epidemiological approach. In N. Morris & M. Tonry (Eds.), *Crime and justice: An annual review of research.* Chicago: University of Chicago Press, 1983.

Monahan, J., & Wexler, D. A definite maybe: Proofs and probability in civil commitment. *Law and Human Behavior,* 1978, *2,* 37–42.

Morse, S. Crazy behavior, morals, and science: An analysis of the mental health legal system. *Southern California Law Review,* 1978, *51,* 527–654.

Petersilia, J., Greenwood, P., & Lavin, M. *Criminal careers of habitual felons.* Santa Monica, Calif.: Rand, 1977.

President's Commission on Mental Health. *Report to the president.* Washington, D.C.: U.S. Government Printing Office, 1978.

Rabkin, J. Criminal behavior of discharged mental patients: A critical appraisal of the research. *Psychological Bulletin,* 1979, *86,* 1–27.

Rawls, J. *A theory of justice.* Cambridge: Harvard University Press, 1972.
Rofman, E. S., Askinazi, C., & Fant, E. The prediction of dangerous behavior in emergency civil commitment. *American Journal of Psychiatry,* 1980, *137,* 1061–1064.
Roth, L., & Ervin, F. Psychiatric care of federal prisoners. *American Journal of Psychiatry,* 1971, *128,* 424–430.
Schwitzgebel, R. L., & Schwitzgebel, R. K. *Law and psychological practice.* New York: Wiley, 1980.
Shinnar, S., & Shinnar, R. The effects of the criminal justice system on the control of crime: A quantitative approach. *Law and Society Review,* 1975, *9,* 581–611.
Sosowsky, L. Explaining the increased arrest rate among mental patients: A cautionary note. *American Journal of Psychiatry,* 1980, *137,* 1602–1605.
State of Maryland. *Maryland's defective delinquency statute—A progress report.* Unpublished manuscript, Department of Public Safety and Correctional Services, 1973.
State of Michigan. *Summary of parolee risk study.* Unpublished manuscript, Department of Corrections, 1978.
Steadman, H. The psychiatrist as a conservative agent of social control. *Social Problems,* 1972, *20,* 262–271.
Steadman, H. A new look at recidivism among Patuxent inmates. *The Bulletin of the American Academy of Psychiatry and the Law,* 1977, *5,* 200–209.
Steadman, H., & Cocozza, J. *Careers of the criminally insane.* Lexington, Mass.: Lexington Books, 1974.
Steadman, H., & Cocozza, J. Selective reporting and the public misconceptions of the criminally insane. *Public Opinion Quarterly,* 1978, *4,* 523–533.
Steadman, H., Cocozza, J., & Melick, M. Explaining the increased crime rate of mental patients: The changing clientele of state hospitals. *American Journal of Psychiatry,* 1978, *135,* 816–820.
Steadman, H., & Halfon, A. The Baxstrom patients: Backgrounds and outcome. *Seminars in Psychiatry,* 1971, *3,* 376–386.
Steadman, H., & Keveles, C. The community adjustment and criminal activity of the Baxstrom patients: 1966–1970. *American Journal of Psychiatry,* 1972, *129,* 304–310.
Stone, A. *Mental health and the law: A system in transition.* (National Institute of Mental Health, Department of Health, Education, and Welfare Publication No. [ADM] 76-176). Washington, D.C.: U.S. Government Printing Office, 1975.
Szasz, T. *Law, Liberty and Psychiatry.* New York: Macmillan, 1963.
Szasz, T. *Psychiatric slavery.* New York: Free Press, 1977.
Tarasoff v. Regents of the University of California, Sup. 131 Cal. Rptr. 14 (1976).
Thornberry, T., and Jacoby, J. *The criminally insane: A community follow-up of mentally ill offenders.* Chicago: University of Chicago Press, 1979.
Twentieth Century Fund. *Fair and certain punishment.* New York: McGraw-Hill, 1976.
Underwood, B. Law and the crystal ball: Predicting behavior with statistical inference and individualized judgment. *Yale Law Journal,* 1979, *88,* 1408–1448.
von Hirsch, A. *Doing justice: The choice of punishments.* New York: Hill & Wang, 1976.
Webster, W. *Crime in the United States—1977.* Washington, D.C.: U.S. Government Printing Office, 1978.
Wolfgang, M. "An Overview of Research into Violent Behavior." Testimony before the House Committee on Science and Technology. 96th Cong., 2d Sess., 1978.
Wolfgang, M., Figlio, R., and Sellin, T. *Delinquency in a birth cohort.* Chicago: University of Chicago Press, 1972.
Zitrin, A., Hardesty, A., Burdock, E., and Drosaman, J. Crime and violence among mental patients. *American Journal of Psychiatry,* 1976, *133,* 142–149.